THE Clothesline REVIEW
MANUAL FOR WRITERS

THE CLOTHESLINE REVIEW MANUAL FOR WRITERS

FIRST PERSON, SINGULAR

MOLLY RAMANUJAN
SHOURI DANIELS

PUBLISHED BY:
THE CLOTHESLINE SCHOOL OF FICTION
5629 Dorchester, Chicago, Illinois 60637

Copyright © 1979, 1985, 1986, 1987 by Molly Ramanujan.
All rights reserved, which includes the right to reproduce
this book or portions thereof in any form whatsoever.
First Printing: 1987
Second Printing: 1994
FOR INFORMATION WRITE TO:
The Clothesline School of Fiction
5629 Dorchester, Chicago IL 60637

COPYRIGHT ACKNOWLEDGMENTS:
"He Died Smiling" by Wilfred Owen: *THE COLLECTED POEMS OF WILFRED OWEN*. Copyright © 1963 by Chatto & Windus, Ltd., Reprinted by permission of New Directions Publishing Corporation.

"Correspondence Between Mr. Harrison in Newcastle and Mr. Sholto Peach Harrison in Hull" and "Man is a Spirit" by Stevie Smith, *Collected Poems*. Copyright © 1922 by Stevie Smith. Reprinted by permission of New Directions Publishing Corporation.

DESIGN: Michael Edwards Communications
TYPOGRAPHY: Sansara Graphics

Printed in the United States of America

TO PAUL PEKIN

CONTENTS

INTRODUCTION 1

PART ONE: Listening for Stories 3

PART TWO: Object, Place, Person, and Event 39

PART THREE: Structure 57

PART FOUR: Actor to Witness 87

PART FIVE: Editing 93

PART SIX: Reading as a Writer 111

Appendix A:
    Biofeedback 117

Appendix B:
    Reading List 119

INTRODUCTION

This manual contains 400 exercises and 200 lessons which will help you find your own fictional voice. If you work through this manual, by the end of the first year you should have a book-length draft of a work of fiction. The method we use is intense, unique, and proven. In the course of the year you will make many discoveries about yourself; not the least of these will be that fiction writing is an exhilarating experience, a natural activity that is a part of your normal everyday life.

The approach to writing fiction will include the following elements:

- Brainstorming. Prewriting exercises.
- Telling stories built around objects through touch, taste, smell, sight, and sound.
- Using the first-person present-tense to achieve immediacy.
- Finding conflict and story line.
- Keeping a writer's notebook of events, dream images, and themes to serve as source material for stories.
- Moving the camera eye.
- Adopting the storyteller's method and voice. Finding the freedom to listen to your way of telling something.
- Moving the camera outward from autobiography to fiction.
- Using the third-person past-tense.
- Learning to read as a writer.

The exercises are programmed in such a way that they progress from the simple to the more complex. Each exercise builds on the previous one. Therefore, it is recommended that you read the manual from cover to cover, then proceed, exercise by exercise, page by page, skipping those exercises that don't seem to open up your material.

I have been using this material to unblock the blocked writer. New writers have gone on to publish and win prizes; experienced writers have found new material. Others say that they have gotten in touch with their sensations and emotions. Participants begin to listen to themselves, and to others; they learn to listen *for* stories, and miraculous processes of discovery are reported. The program is holistic. In the process of finding their own voices, participants claim that they have been detoxified in more ways than one.

The work of healing done by holistic doctors and psychiatrists is made more complete through writing these images from real life. Whatever is a minus in real life becomes a plus on the page. What seemed unacceptable or incomplete or damaged becomes a new source of strength. Since our brainstorming involves sensations, ideas, and emotions (*soma, pneuma,* and *psyche*), there are special rewards that come from finding connections between the fragments we surface.

Every Sunday, participants from the workshops give a dramatic reading of an original anthology of stories at the Woodlawn Tap, 1172 East 55th Street, Chicago, Illinois, from 3:00 to 4:30 P.M. These stories vary in length from a quarter of a page to five or six pages. We believe that a long story is a series of short images. In our program, we go after the short movements which later join together and become longer pieces. As soon as we have a unit of narration that can stand by itself, has a basic emotion, and catches a moment of change, we hang it up on our imaginary clothesline. When the ink is dry, we take it down and read it to an audience. They tell us that our images are dramatic and true.

We find that writing is as much fun as our Illinois writer, Ernest Hemingway, said it was. Several participants have given up alcohol, coffee, cigarettes. Their day begins to have more space and time for brainstorming. As the writing releases energy, more things are accomplished each day in whatever they undertake.

As when we dream, so also when we write, our imagination is like the ocean with every kind of fish in it. We find that everyone is creative, and that there is no dearth of powerful stories. We can write during the day as easily and as powerfully as we dream at night.

LISTENING FOR STORIES PART 1

Storytelling is intrinsic to man. Our best stories occur at night, and we find that our dreams have a narrative structure (a relationship between the parts and the whole). This is because the dreamer is autonomous; he is the author. There is a unique and seemingly wordless way in which things come back to us from the past. If we listen carefully to the order in which an event enters our minds, we can learn something about narrative forms.

Organic form is in the material. We don't impose form on the material; form is inseparable from the way we perceive something. Yet, most of us have to train ourselves to listen to ourselves. Some of us have stopped listening to ourselves early in childhood. If we wish to become fiction writers, we must begin by listening to the way in which events surface in our minds. We can do this by jotting down rapidly thing after thing in the order in which each appears. Each time we note something, by association, other events will surface. We must listen *for* stories. Eudora Welty writes, "Long before I wrote stories, I listened for stories. Listening for them is something more acute than listening to them."[1]

In infancy, we first felt things before we found the words for the feelings; we wrote much later. In writing, we want to retrace this process. If we do this, our writing will be true. To begin with, we have to do sensation exercises somewhat in the way we practice scales when learning to play the piano.

KEEPING A JOURNAL

Each time an image enters your mind, you must learn to make quick notes in your journal. If you don't make a note, you will lose the material, for it won't visit you in the same sequence again. If you note down the sequence in which the event comes to you, the material becomes more useable in your fiction. Later, you will learn to donate some of these journal entries to your fictional characters.

A journal is different from a diary. Your journal is a "writer's notebook," a quarry for the building blocks of your future stories. This chapter will teach you to make entries in your journal. Some of these may not be fleshed out fully, but they are the ABC of fiction. Each time you jot down something, it will continue to work in your subconscious and generate other images. At first you may not see the connections between one entry and another, but when you have a sufficient number of them, some of the entries will join hands with others to become longer movements.

1. New York Times Book Review, October 9, 1983.

Primary Images

EARLIEST MEMORY

We asked Saul Bellow for his earliest memory. He smiled as if to say, "That's an easy one." He had two early memories; they went together. In the first one, he is about a year and a half, and in the second he's a year older.

He is sitting before a fire, watching the play of flames. He crawls toward it and pulls out a log, and the burning end pits his leg. "I still carry the scar," he says, pointing to his left leg, mid-calf.

His mother bundles him in a snow suit and asks him to go outside and build snow castles. Each day he builds a new castle for his mother. There is no one else in the backyard. His fingers and toes are freezing.

In some of the more powerful images in Mr. Bellow's fiction, several of his heroes—Augie March, Henderson, Herzog, Citrine—are burnt by beauty, or left out in the cold, even as they build "castles."

EXERCISE:

- WHAT IS YOUR EARLIEST MEMORY?
- Write it in the present tense. Focus on an object. Follow what happened next. Do not stretch or pad. Have faith in the material that surfaces. Do not interfere with the sequence. Remove all explanations. Do not directly name the emotion. Let the reader feel the emotion.

PREWRITING EXERCISE:

- Who else is present at the time of your earliest memory?
- Make a list of persons.
- Who is the most important to you?
- Think of inanimate objects that come back to you when you think of this person: for example, mother's dressing-table, father's closet, grandfather's tool box. In each instance, consult your feelings and see if you feel pleasure or pain.
- Place pluses and minuses against each object.

ONE-OF-A-KIND TANGIBLES AND SENSATIONS

Inanimate Objects

EXERCISES:

- ○ Think of a pleasant smell you associate with a person who was most important to you. Think of something that was not pleasant.

    Write it down in the present tense.

    Read it over and eliminate all explanations. Remove adjectives and adverbs.

- ○ Let your mind go over tangible things you can touch and taste and smell and see and hear.

    You are in a strange place: let your five senses find inanimate objects.

    Make notes.

- ○ Touch/taste/smell. These are the more private of your senses. Through these, try to get back into those moments of change in the past.

    Put down short movements of what comes into your mind.

    Do not interfere with the integrity of your seeing.

A MOVEMENT FROM FAMILIAR TO UNFAMILIAR:

- ○ Let us think of a movement from familiar to unfamiliar.

    See an object that is familiar and then something that happens that is unfamiliar.

    Focus on the object and write down what happens next, in the present tense.

    A good image is more than a description. It means something to your listener. It has a basic human emotion: anger, jealousy, fear.

    Do not name the emotion. Do not use the words anger, jealousy, fear.

Opposites: THE PLUS AND THE MINUS

Light and dark, pleasure and pain, real and unreal, familiar and unfamiliar, a plus and a minus: opposites and contraries go together on a page.

- If something pleasant comes into your mind, think of something unpleasant. Make a note of both.
- If something familiar comes into your mind, think of something unfamiliar. Make a note of both.

Learn to make quick notes. Opposites give energy to the writing.

Find a moment when something happened, and look for opposites.

WARM-UP EXERCISES:

- Through touch, taste, or smell suggest tangibles for the following opposites:

OPENED / CLOSED	EARLY / LATE
IN / OUT	MORNING / EVENING
UP / DOWN	NOON / MIDNIGHT
NARROW / WIDE	WEEKDAY / WEEKEND
STRAIGHT / CROOKED	

- As soon as you think of an object, get in touch with a basic emotion that it evokes. Do not name that emotion. Focus on the object and note what happened next, exactly as it surfaces in your mind. Accept what comes to you. Do not pad. Be true to the way something pops into your mind. Wordiness implies that you are not really listening to yourself. Notice that your dreams are never wordy.

MORE WARM-UPS: FEELING THE TENSION OF OPPOSITES

- CLEAR / FOGGY   SMOOTH / GRAINY

  FAIR / DARK   BLACK / WHITE

  Focus each time on an inanimate object. See it, feel it, and follow the sequence of what happened next.

- LOUD / SOFT   SHARP / SOFT

  HARSH / SOOTHING   CAUTIOUS / BOLD

  STEADY / INTERMITTENT

  A train whistle. The garbage truck at dawn. The roar of a mountain river. Each time a sensation returns to you, see who else is present. Ask yourself: What happened next? Make notes.

- FRESH / MOULDY   STRONG / WEAK

  SWEET / SOUR   CLEAN / DIRTY

  Feel these opposites through your senses; focus on tangibles. We want one-of-a-kind objects. Each time, feel the basic emotion. Make notes.

- Think of your earliest period and think of:

  HOT / COLD   SOFT / HARD

  ROUGH / SMOOTH   WET / DRY

  SHARP / DULL   SOLID / LIQUID

  Look for tangibles for each of the above. Think of these as present, here and now, in front of you. Put a "plus" or a "minus" sign next to each tangible by consulting your feelings.

Opening Up the Opposites:

SHORT MOVEMENTS

AN IMAGE:

- ○ Each of these tangibles is one-of-a-kind, and occurs in a one-time action. If habitual actions come to mind, accept them, and then look for the one time when something unexpected happened.

- ○ Focus on an object, and write down rapidly as if taking dictation from the voice inside you. Do not interfere with the sequence in which something enters your mind. Do not explain anything.

- ○ Reread, and remove all adjectives and adverbs. Go over your verbs. Are they in the present tense? How many of them are action verbs? Is there a difference between beginning, middle, and end?

HANG UP THE SHORT MOVEMENTS ON AN IMAGINARY CLOTHESLINE

A long story is a series of short movements. We believe that the short movements come to us singly and at different times. Each time an event surfaces, we take down notes rapidly. Each entry works in the subconscious, and each object that is recalled brings to mind other objects. As soon as we have a movement that can stand by itself without explanation, to which a reader can respond without help from the writer, we hang it up on our clothesline for the ink to dry. After we have done hundreds of such short movements, some of them will join together and make a single unit of narration.

Prewriting and writing exercises: for several weeks, you will be making lists. Every now and again, an entry will open up, and reveal to you an object, a place, a person, or event through one or more of your senses. When an entry opens up, listen to yourself with everything you've got, and take down dictation exactly as the objects and the sequence of what happens next enter your mind.

EXERCISE:

- ○ From among the objects that surfaced, choose one that will open up when you ask yourself: "What happened next?" Write in the present tense. Go over what you have written and remove all explanations. Do not try to be "literary." Be true to the voice inside you. Just follow the sequence in which the object entered your mind. Follow the object.

> OBJECTS ARE TAKEN IN THROUGH THE FIVE SENSES:
>
> TOUCH   TASTE   SIGHT   SOUND   SMELL
>
> Object: What is the basic emotion?
>
> To begin with, choose short segments of time: a half-hour, an hour.
>
> Catch a moment of change.

EXERCISE:

- Pick an object that has the strongest pull. Something that has both a "plus" and a "minus." Feel the conflict. Focus on the object and follow it. Put down, in the present tense, what comes to you. Do not try to make a story out of it. Be true to the feeling and do not interfere with the sequence in which it enters your mind.

A SHORT ENTRY

There's the knife with the uneven edge with which Uncle Jay took out the pebble from the hoof of my pony. Uncle Jay's hair smelled of gunpowder after his wife ran away with the carpenter who came to build the new barn.

MORE EXERCISES:

- Think of a time when you touched something you should not have touched. What happened next? Write in the present tense. Go over what you have written. Remove all the adjectives and adverbs. Cut out any explanations. Write lean.

- Follow the inanimate objects; see these objects through the lens of a particular emotion. Do not explain anything. Think in the present tense, as if it is happening right now. Later you may translate it into the simple past, which is the usual narrative tense. Do not set up the scene or write description for the sake of description. In each and every instance, there is usually more than one problem, and each thing on the page is doing more than one thing. Think of a person who is angry, think of an object you saw this person destroy. What happened next? Don't try to be logical or rational. Follow the sequence.

EXERCISE:

○ Read the story "Paper Pills" from Sherwood Anderson's *Winesburg, Ohio*. Put the book aside. Now try to recall all the objects in the story. You will notice:

- That you can recall most of the objects, and
- That if you take away the objects you don't have the same story.

Let each entry be a one-time action. We begin the telling by focusing on a one-of-a-kind object. For example, we're thinking of mouldy/fresh. We want to think of that particular piece of cherry pie Mary received in the mail from cousin Tim on the warmest day in ten years. The cherry pie tells us something about cousin Tim, while at the same time allowing us to keep our minds open. A good image is like a widening gyre; it alerts the reader to a great range of possibilities.

SUBJECT / OBJECT

Objects give the reader space to enter the story. The objects objectify the subjective experience and make the story believable. Objects are recognizable and communicable. The reader has a sense of the life on the page as if (s)he were experiencing it first hand.

EXAMPLE OF A TANGIBLE:

In Atlanta, a man is about to be executed for the brutal murder of a neighbor. He orders a dozen fresh oysters for his last supper. The jailers ask him if he wants some more, and he says, "No." A reporter wants to know why he ordered oysters, and he says, "I'd never tasted them before." The reporter says, "Oysters are an acquired taste."

This is our example of what T. S. Eliot called "The Objective Correlative." We might say, as John Keats did, ". . . the sedge is withered from the Lake and no birds sing," to suggest the desolation of the rejected man's world.

EXERCISES:

○ Read out to someone what you have written, and you will find that your listener can recall every object in your writing. Similarly, after you have read a story, preferably a classic, try to recall each object in the story. When reading, mark all the inanimate objects; circle the ones that have a dramatic function.

○ If you were to divide your life into different parts, where would you make the divisions? Make a list. Find as many objects as you can for each of the divisions.

OPENING UP AN ENTRY:

○ Think of the first major change in your life. Look for the moment of change. Find an object. See the place. Catch a short movement from familiar to unfamiliar, or vice versa. Feel the emotion. Write in the present tense. Remove all explanations. Change the verbs to active where necessary.

A SENSATION EXERCISE:

○ What is your weakest sense? Make a note of it. Now make a list of all the times you have been angry. Use your weakest sense and look for objects that were present at the time when you were angry. Write rapidly and open up some of these.

BRAINSTORMING FOR IMAGES:

○ Divide your life according to persons in your life. Select the ones who were the most important. Brainstorm for objects you associate with each of them. Make lists. Put pluses and minuses against each of the objects. Get in touch with a basic emotion through one or more of your senses as you consider those that have both a plus and a minus and save the rest.

○ Look over the objects that have both a plus and a minus. Feel the basic emotion. Pick the one that comes back to you and open it up. Rapidly tell what happened. Do not explain anything. Do not strain for effect. Be true to the object; let it lead you to what happened next. Do not try to write a *story*. Just follow the object and the sequence. Stop when that particular sequence is over.

○ Look for the objects with both pleasure and pain. Try to open these up. See the place, the person, the event; focus on an object and plunge in. Do not try to explain or set up the scene—that kind of justification is of no interest to the reader. Remember, you are a storyteller. When in doubt, think of a fairy tale.

○ Look once more at the divisions you made of your life. See if there is any pattern or repetition in the division. Look for objects that come up as you think of a moment of change.

GIVE THE READER SOME WORK

Some objects on the page have a luminous quality, like the chalice in "The Sisters" (the opening story in *Dubliners* by James Joyce). In that story, the chalice functions three times, when it is (1) empty, (2) broken, (3) buried. The reader makes the connections. The writer does not explain. These three aspects cover the movement of the story. There is a collaboration between the writer and the reader. An easier example can be found in "Paper Pills" in *Winesburg, Ohio* by Sherwood Anderson. The twisted apples with their core of sweetness are what Dr. Reefy is to the tall dark girl.

FROM START TO FINISH
OUR IMAGES ARE AIMED AT A LISTENER

How can we make objects illuminate a page? First of all, we must not interfere with the reader's ability to see, hear, taste, smell, touch, and judge. In fake writing, we may find such a sentence as "She fingered the beads delicately." In our view, this object comes to us at two removes: the word "delicately" interposes the author's comment between us and the woman, and the woman comes between us and the beads. We don't have any work to do. If you begin a movement with sunlight "seeping in through the window," or "making crazy quilt patterns," or some such thing, you may be sure you are faking it. We don't hear your voice; such sentences can be written by anyone.

The one-of-a-kind objects from the real world and the basic emotions felt by human beings everywhere go together in our fiction to create authentic images that hook the reader's attention. In our kind of writing, we would like to wake the reader up. To do this, we must respect the reader's integrity by avoiding labels. We provide objects that have a dramatic function in the story. It's the reader who does the labeling.

EXERCISES: SENSATIONS AND OBJECTS

Though we use words, we want to be wordless. This can be achieved by moving the camera eye outward, focusing on an object, and seeing what happened next. In each of the following exercises, choose a short segment of time when something happened. Go for the moments of conflict. Follow the sequence in which something enters your mind.

THINK OF:

- Your strongest sense: touch, taste, smell.

- Something you touched in a moment of panic.

- Something you tasted for the last time.

- A smell that reminds you of a person who was once important to you.

- An object that reminds you of something you heard.

- An object that reminds you of something you saw.

- An object that you wish you had kept.

- An object that was wasted on the wrong person.

- An object that caused a rift between two persons.

- *There was a man and he was mad*
  And he ran up the steeple,
  And there he cut his nose off
  And he flung it at the people.[2]

CAN YOU THINK OF SOMETHING MAD THAT SOMEONE DID?

2. Anonymous.

FICTION DOES NOT MEAN FICTITIOUS

The difference between what happens in real life and what happens in fiction is a result of the technique of fiction. The fiction writer moves his camera eye outward. He presents the objects, the places, the persons, and the events in such a way that anyone who looks at it long enough will begin to see not only the visible part of the event, but also the hidden part. In real life, each viewer has his version of what happened.

Fiction is the art of moving outward. The mind of the character is a very narrow place for a fiction writer to settle in. The camera eye (I) of the narrator should be focused outward on the tangible.

THE READER'S RESPONSE

The spectator in a real life event might be subjective in his responses, but the technique of fiction makes the reader's response more objective. In real life, we are moved to action by an event; when reading fiction, the reader can exercise a free play of the mind and contemplate every aspect; he can read and reread. The fiction writer makes visible on the page not only what was visible in real life, but that which was hidden from view.

BEGINNINGS

We want to hook the reader's attention. If the opening sentence gives the reader some work, it is likely to entice him/her to read on.

Read the opening sentence of George Orwell's *1984*. This is an ideal opening. It gives the reader work by alerting him/her. "It was a bright cold day in April, and the clocks were striking thirteen."[3] Write the beginning of each exercise and try it on people who are *not* good listeners, and see if you can get them *hooked*. Rehearse the opening lines of your stories. Collect a few great beginnings from the classics as your touchstones.

---

3. George Orwell (New York: Octopus/Heinemann, 1980), p. 743.

THE FREEDOM OF THE FICTION WRITER

The values of fiction are the same as in life but with an enormous difference for the writer. What is unpleasant in life becomes strong and valuable on the page. Something that is dangerous in real life ceases to be dangerous on the page. In life, a thief is bad and a murderer is worse; in literature, a thief is good and a murderer is better. Who said that? (Was it Schiller?) A house on fire in real life creates panic. A house on fire in a work of fiction is an object of contemplation. There is no threat in it. Literature is created out of a free play of the imagination.

An entry won't work as fiction if the writer is trying to be partisan or sectarian. The best images of fiction are open-ended. They give the reader a chance to weigh the pros and cons and debate right and wrong. It is the reader who arrives at conclusions, not the writer.

UNITS OF TIME:
CHOOSING A SHORT SEGMENT OF TIME WHEN SOMETHING HAPPENED

IN BRAINSTORMING FOR AN IMAGE, WE MAY FOCUS ON:

TOUCH   TASTE   SIGHT   SOUND   SMELL

Inanimate Object — Place — Person — Event

SEGMENT OF TIME WHEN SOMETHING HAPPENED

ENDINGS

We write the endings first. We want no explanation in the ending. No adjectives. No adverbs. We want to convey an open-ended moment without words. We want the object to communicate the basic emotion of the ending. Learn by heart the last three lines of Hemingway's novel *A Farewell to Arms* as a touchstone.

SHORT MOVEMENTS:

- Think of things that you can no longer touch or taste or smell or hear or see.

    Make a list. Put down as many one liners as you can and save them for later use.

- Get in touch with your five senses. Brainstorm for familiar and unfamiliar sensations: touch, taste, smell, sight, and sound. Go back to an earlier period; find a moment which keeps coming back to you. Find a sensation that takes you from familiar to unfamiliar or vice versa.

LISTENING CREATIVELY:

- Get in touch with the five senses. Brainstorm for pleasant and unpleasant: touch, taste, smell, sight, and sound.

    Find a moment that changed from ungenerous to generous. Write rapidly and without self-consciousness.

    Listen to yourself. Most of us have stopped listening to ourselves. If we train ourselves to listen creatively, what entertains us will entertain others. First you have to learn to listen to your own voice, and only then can you really listen to other people.

- Think of a person and think of objects you associate with this person. Grade the objects according to the strength of the emotion. Choose the strongest.

    Give each event a segment of time — five minutes, a half-hour.

    These short movements will fit into larger movements later on.

- See a familiar person in an unfamiliar place. Focus on an object. Get in touch with a basic emotion. The stronger the emotion, the more powerful the image. The emotion gives unity to the telling. Choose the material you know best. Do not strain for effect. Originality lies in the sequence in which each thing enters your mind. Trust the voice inside you.

- Go over the objects once more. Put down the sensations next to the objects.

MOVING OUTWARD: FOCUSING ON OBJECTS

- Find an object with a movement from pleasant to unpleasant.

    Write rapidly and then read over.

    Strike out any explanations. See that the sentences do not bury important action verbs in subordinate clauses.

    Rearrange the words so that the emphasis is right.

- Think of a person other than yourself.

    Focus on an object over which there is conflict.

    Feel the emotion, follow the object—be aware of the plus and minus; write rapidly in the sequence in which it enters your mind.

    Go over what you write. Cut out explanations; give the reader the freedom to judge, to choose, to intuit, to understand. Avoid labels.

THE BASIC EMOTION GIVES UNITY TO AN IMAGE

- Put down basic emotions, the ones you have not attempted.

    Find objects for each.

    Find the places, the persons, the events.

    Choose a segment of time; break it into shorter segments.

    Choose the tiny segment that constitutes the ending. Start writing the ending. Read out the ending. See if a listener can get the movement, the emotion. See if there are any explanations. Remove the explanations. Remove wordiness. Is it open-ended; will it continue to grow in the mind of the listener?

    Now write the event.

    Go back to the beginning and see if you can remove explanations; see if there is a hint of a problem or mystery or conflict, or any kind of hook to make the reader wonder what happened, and what happened next.

    Read out the whole.

POINT OF VIEW

Point of view is nothing but where the emotion is coming from. If we understand the first-person point of view thoroughly, then all other points of view will have depth. If we try the third person before we have fully explored the first person, we may not discover the full range of what we can do. To begin with, we are the actors in our writing, but as we learn to move outward, we become witnesses; when an event is totally witnessed, we have the third person.

DIRECT AND INDIRECT SPEECH

EXERCISES:

- ○ Put down single sentences of direct quotes of what you heard others say. Make two columns of WHAT OTHERS SAID:

    Column A: WHAT I UNDERSTOOD THEN

    Column B: WHAT I DIDN'T UNDERSTAND TILL MUCH LATER

In putting down dialogue credits, put down simply, "Grandmother said," or "Uncle Jerry said." Do not put in words like "insisted," "persisted," "asserted," or other such descriptions. Such descriptions destroy the illusion of overhearing direct speech.

Do not record every word uttered. We want to select choice bits in order to create the illusion of direct speech. Dialogue is more useful in scenes of conflict. Learn to vary the pace; do not go on with a good thing until it becomes boring. Quit while it's going strong and slant into indirect narration, as you would when telling it to someone.

- ○ Read "Two Sisters" in *Dubliners* and see how and why Joyce alternates between direct and indirect speech. Write an exchange of words you overheard between two persons who were fighting over an object.

In writing dialogue, be true to each person's script so that they don't sound alike. Dialogue should not sound like a debate. Feel free to include the irrational, the illogical, or the unexpected, so long as it's true to the speaker's emotion. Study the opening chapter of Jane Austen's *Pride and Prejudice*.

FORM

Form is intrinsic to the material. We discover form by listening to the order in which an event surfaces in the mind. This method encourages you to recognize creativity. What gives unity is the basic emotion. The stronger the emotion, the more memorable the event is for the reader. Those events that have opposites, a movement from a plus to minus or minus to plus, will teach us structure or form.

CONFLICT AND STORY

A conflict, or the tension of opposites, releases energy. Something happens, something is done. There's a consequence. What is done may not be rational, but the consequence is logical. The sequence of what happened next gives us the beginning, middle, and end of an entry.

A good telling has in the middle of it a mystery. In writing, we are expressing our awe and wonder. We do not explain; we are witnesses. The reader is left to figure things out.

EXERCISES:

- Make a list of people who have filled you with a sense of mystery. Think of places that have this quality.

- Think of something that happened that no one understood, which only you understood.

  Focus on an object. See the place. Write rapidly.

  Go over what you have written; remove all explanations. Check the verbs. Look at your opening lines, and then look up the opening of George Orwell's *1984*.

- Choose a short segment of time when something happened. Write it down rapidly by focusing on an object.

  Write the ending first. See that the ending has no explanations, no adjectives or adverbs. Do not stretch; do not pad. Write lean.

  Go over the verbs. Make sure that the "subject" or the "action verb" is not in a subordinate clause.

  Try it on someone and see if they feel like entering the story through the back door.

REMEMBER, WE ARE STORYTELLERS WITHOUT CONFLICT, THERE IS NO STORY

For those who are writing their first book-length work of fiction, we recommend that the conflict be between two persons, or between a person and an institution, or with some visible thing outside himself. Hamlet-like internal vacillations are never successful and are invariably boring unless the writer has mastered the art of telling a story that is packed with action and which can be mimed. Shakespeare's thinking hero is also paradoxically one of the most active acting-out characters.

EXERCISE:

- Study conflict in a family quarrel. Make one person do something that everyone present can see; note what happens next. Do not explain; plunge in by focusing on an object.

Without separation, there can be no consciousness; individuation is not possible without conflict. For fiction to work on the page, there has to be at least one problem, which in its turn creates another problem, and so on till a change takes place for better or worse. Without conflict, characterization is not possible.

In the opening lines of *Anna Karenina*, Tolstoy tells us, "All happy families resemble one another, but each unhappy family is unhappy in its own way."[4] Choose a person who is unhappy in his own way, and then look for a moment of change.

CATCHING A MOMENT OF CHANGE

In fiction, as in life, we are not stuck in a fixed moment. If we take even the smallest segment of time, we can find in it some difference between the beginning, the middle, and the end. We want to catch moments of change, moving from happiness to unhappiness, or familiar to unfamiliar.

An image entry should be able to stand by itself, while at the same time allowing further movement. Read out your endings to someone and see if they can intuit the movement without further explanation. In testing a beginning, see if the choice of material is intrinsically interesting to the listener.

We use a particular concrete instance, a one-of-a-kind object or a one-time action, but we do it in such a way as to make it universal, something that can be felt anywhere at any time.

---

4. Leo Tolstoy, *Anna Karenina* (London: Oxford University Press, 1965), p. 1.

In order to make the hidden part accessible to the reader in a believable way, we have to get in touch with our emotions somewhat in the way an actor has to get in touch with his emotions while acting. It is the emotion that gives unity to the piece. We may play a murder scene with the emotions of a mean killer, or we may take on those of a noble one. We have to dig deep into our consciousness to put into the movement something out of our experience. Yet we never forget that we are entertainers and that we wear many masks.

We are not attempting to write an epic at one sitting. We want to catch a moment of change when something happened. The connections between one segment and another will emerge as we go along.

AN EXAMPLE OF A SHORT IMAGE

A participant in my workshop tells me that in the convent there was a holy water rag which was used to mop up spilled holy water. Once, seeing that no one was looking, she ran down the hallway and found some toilet paper. She mopped up the holy water and flushed it down the toilet. This short unit foreshadows an event to be narrated, in which she leaves the convent and gets married. Each of the units that go to make up a longer unit can stand by itself. Each has a beginning, a middle, and an end. In this sense, our shortest movements and our longest have the same strength.

EXERCISES:

- Look over what you have done up to now; circle each object (i.e., holy water rag) that has a function in an entry.

- Pick an event where there is a difference between the beginning, the middle, and the end. Write rapidly; go over what you have written, and rewrite clauses that begin with "because," "as," "when," "while"; watch out for "always," "usually," and other habitual tracks—we want something that happened one time and we are most interested in one-of-a-kind objects.

- Think of an event in which you change from being cautious to being bold. Focus on an object. See what happened next. Do not try to change material to fit the mode of what you think a story "ought" to be. Be true to the object. What you write will work on the page. Write rapidly and in the present tense. Read over and remove all adjectives, adverbs, and explanations from what you have written.

YOU ARE THE AUTHORITY: THERE IS NO ONE ABOVE YOU

LEARNING FROM OURSELVES

We can learn from ourselves by listening to the order in which an event enters our minds when we try to recall it. We don't do this in the ordinary way of memory, but as if it were happening before our eyes. Another source would be our dreams.

Unless we are true to the objects, the reader cannot touch, taste, smell, see, hear, or judge. To understand our method, to learn how objects function, we should study our dreams. There are people who think they don't dream. Please try the following experiment and you will find that you not only dream, but that your dreams are more brilliant than anything you think or write when awake. Before going to sleep, put by your bedside table a notebook and a pencil and tell yourself that you're going to note down objects from your dreams first thing in the morning.

OUR DREAMS ARE MADE OF OBJECTS FROM THE REAL WORLD

Even a few objects will make the dream accessible to you. When you wake up, accept whatever remains of the dream, and enter it in your dream book. Each day your recall will improve. Gradually there will be a curious relationship between what you create and what you dream. The dreamer is autonomous, like the author. There is no one above him or her.

LEONARDO DA VINCI'S RECURRING DREAM

Leonardo da Vinci says in his notebooks:

"This writing distinctly about the kites seems to be my destiny, because among the first recollections of my infancy it seemed to me that, as I was in my cradle, a kite came to me and opened my mouth with its tail, and struck me several times with its tail inside my lips."[5]

---

5. *The Notebooks of Leonardo da Vinci,* Pamela Taylor (New York: Mentor Books, 1960), p. 217.

EXERCISES:

- Write down in the present tense a recurring dream. Do not stretch; do not pad. Follow the sequence. Organic form is intrinsic to the material. The form of the story can be found in the order in which the event enters the mind. Do not interfere with the sequence. Do not mention the word "dream" in your piece.

- Make a list of dreams you remember, yours or other people's. Look for objects in each dream. Look for a dream that occurs on days when you or someone else has been in some kind of trouble.

IN DREAMS BEGINS REALITY

Each day, notice how the dreams of the night before color the day's events, just as the real-life events color the dreams. As you get deeper into this manual, you will find some of the writing exercises turning up in your dreams. One participant, a filmmaker, finds himself in a room with no light. Looking for a light switch in a rowboat, he finds a flashlight at the bottom of the boat, and when he turns it on, he sees the family album opened with the picture of the missing grandmother and other luminous objects. On the bedside table in the morning he finds a note which says, "Buy batteries."

HIDDEN KNOWLEDGE

We know more than we think we do. Even a lightweight, like Lockwood in *Wuthering Heights*, knows more in his dreams than he seems capable of intuiting during the day. In the two dreams in Chapter Three, he seems to know more about Catherine Earnshaw and her world than he had actually learned from reading her marginalia or meeting Heathcliff.

Lockwood is a superficial gentleman from London with easy ways of thinking and feeling. But his nightlife shows him to be much closer to the elemental world of Catherine and Heathcliff. Our dreams are nearer the themes of great literature than anything we can think of during the day. Things happen in our dreams. The camera eye is always turned outward in our dreams.

ARCHETYPES

In our dreams there are certain archetypal motifs—of being lost in a forest or a desert, of separation by floods or earthquakes, of being caught in storms at sea, of the day the sun or the moon stood still, of waking up as an insect, of killer plants, of ancestral postures, of bloody acts of revenge or betrayal, of compulsions and repetitions, etc. So also, in our themes, there are certain basic movements and motifs.

Write your dream in the present tense. Do not say it is a dream. Write it as if it is happening. Take particular note of those dreams which, upon waking, confuse you as to what is actual and what is in the dream. As in dreams, so in writing, if you lose the sequence, the entry becomes flat and loses its magic and meaning.

MOVEMENT FROM REAL TO UNREAL OR FROM UNREAL TO REAL

EXERCISES:

- Write about: a dream that had something in it that happened to you or someone else in real life; a real life event that mimicked something you or someone else dreamed about. Avoid analysis or explanations. Explanations make the telling prosaic or essayistic. Are you familiar with the prophetic dreams in the Old Testament? Look up the dreams in Emily Bronte's *Wuthering Heights*.

- Think of something small that appeared enormous or vice versa. If it is from a dream, do not mention that it is from a dream. See it in the present tense. Think of a place you revisited that looked small. Think of persons who suddenly appeared small.

- Think of a dream in which someone died. See the object, the person, the event. Write lean. Do not try to be literary.

- There is a person in your life about whom disaster images come to your mind frequently. Make a note of the scene each time this happens. Each time, make a note of the circumstances that trigger these flashes about this person. Do not explain. Respect the mysterious way in which things turn up. Watch the process. Make a note.

- Look over your dream notebook which you keep by your bedside and circle all the objects which have a dramatic function. Learn about objects from your dreams.

PATTERNS AND ECHOES

EXERCISES:

- SEEN / UNSEEN   REAL / UNREAL

  PRESENT / ABSENT   LIVING / DEAD

  Think of these words and invite objects into your mind. In each instance, think of the basic emotion. Think of short movements. Jot down rapidly what enters the mind. Read over and remove all explanations.

  In each instance we try to re-enter the moment as if we were reliving it. We do this through the senses. We narrate the event by focusing on objects. Trust the object and it will never betray the truth of the moment. If we leave out the objects, reality on the page would be what one practitioner described as "self-regarding."

EXERCISES:

- Do you have a recurring memory? Focus on an object and write it down exactly in the sequence in which it enters your mind. Do not interfere with the order in which it surfaces in your mind. Omit, if possible, adjectives and adverbs. Think of an event which recurred. Think of the first time it happened. Think of the next time, and the next. Next to each entry put down an object that comes back to you.

  At the heart of every image there is a sense of something mysterious. Something that can't be explained away. We note the plus and the minus. We follow what happens next. We put in *who* said *what* to *whom*; but an image is more than the sum of its parts. It is in this sense that it differs from a news story.

UNIVERSALS: WHAT ANY READER ANYWHERE CAN EXPERIENCE

Our memory is like the ocean itself. It has fish of every kind and of every size. We want to begin with the little ones. Write a few lines, half a page at a time, and then we'll know when to use them. We want to know our range, and we want to feel our depths. We can begin by making a few more lists.

Unlike real life, the life on the page cannot harm us. Experiences that are painful in real life become pleasurable in the act of translating them into fiction. We learn to share the objects and events we have encountered by donating them to the characters we create.

EXERCISES:

- Make a list of basic emotions: jealousy, love, hate, fear, anger, despair, anxiety. Add a few more. Look for the ones you feel frequently and place objects next to each emotion. Go back to childhood and find objects.

SENSATIONS: THE BASIC BUILDING BLOCKS OF FICTION

- Think of a sensation that comes back to you from childhood. List all the places where you felt that sensation. Make lists of objects and one-liners.

- Go back to an earlier period when your sensations were most acute. List all the times you got into trouble by breaking a rule of the house or school. Invite tangibles through your five senses; focus on the clearest thing and be a witness to what happened next. Make rapid notes. Read "An Encounter" in James Joyce's *Dubliners*. Retell it to another person and see if you can hold this person's attention.

- Take two units of time, the first time you experienced something and the last time you experienced the same thing, and put them together with the use of a common object. For example, the very first time you saw a snake and the last time you saw a snake. Note the sensations that come back to you.

THE PRIVATE AND THE PUBLIC

In fiction, sight is the primary sense, but the more private senses are even more memorable on the page. Each of us has our strongest and weakest sense. By alternating between the strongest and the weakest, we lessen the gap. Go back to a time when your senses were most acute. Focus on a particular moment and invite sensations, particularly touch and smell. Make notes.

- Touch, taste, and smell are the private senses; sight and sound are the more public. The Greeks thought that sight was the noblest, but we know that for some people, sound is the noblest. Touch is the most extensive. When we lose touch, we are dead. Read T. S. Eliot's "Preludes" and underline all the sensations, particularly touch and smell.

A MOVEMENT FROM FAMILIAR TO UNFAMILIAR SUGGESTS THE AWE AND WONDER AT THE HEART OF A GOOD IMAGE

○ Go back to childhood and smell something dead: flowers, grass, plants, trees, a mouse. The movement is from familiar to unfamiliar.

In private life, what smells good to one person may smell bad to another. For instance, the smell of curry is offensive to anyone except a curry addict. There can be no consensus on touch, taste, and smell, but in writing fiction we learn to translate the private into the public. In fiction, it is the context, the process, the situation, or the basic emotion that affirms a private sensation. There is a place, a person or persons, and an event. The more private of the senses are related to character and situation, and they make visible on the page something that cannot be communicated any other way.

In terms of single lines, we begin by putting two sensations together, things that are dissimilar but have something in common (i.e., we could put smell and taste together). Here are two examples from the journal of a 12-year-old: "My mouth tastes like the inside of my sneakers." "My cat smells of corn cobs."

We do not go after experimentation for its own sake. If there is no consensus of the commonly felt meaning for different kinds of readers (be they Eskimos, East Indians, or Northern Europeans), which at the same time allows for different levels of interpretation, the writing would be less than great. In our program, we do two things at the same time: we try to listen to the way things enter our minds while at the same time aiming our stories at a listener in a way that he will be able to see what we see, feel what we feel. By writing without explanation, by focusing on objects, by looking for the plus and minus, we make possible multiple levels of meaning.

MORE SENSATION EXERCISES:

○ Choose an hour of the day, such as 6:00 P.M., and record, through your senses, one-liners about what happens at that hour at a place that's familiar to you. See T. S. Eliot's "Preludes."

○ Look out of the window. What kind of day is it? Sunny? Dark? Cold? Windy? Warm? Humid? Is it raining or snowing? Let your mind go over what happened on a day such as the one you are now contemplating. Make quick notes.

○ Think of a person whom you knew as a child, but who is no more; think of all the sensations you associate with this person. Tell something you overheard about this person. See the person who said it. See the place. Without explaining anything, invent details, but be faithful to the emotion.

GO OVER EACH PIECE YOU HAVE WRITTEN AND REMOVE ALL ADJECTIVES AND ADVERBS

○ Brainstorm for first-time sensations. Your first experience of a mountain, a desert, a sea. Your first ride on a bicycle. The first money you earned. Your first train ride. The first time you were by yourself in a strange place.

○ Think that you have a movie camera and are moving around trying to catch all you can of what is happening. Think of a person and a sound. A person and a phrase. A person and an object. A person and a place. A person and another person. Each time, feel the emotion—select the ones that have a conflict. Without explaining, write the endings first. Then write the middle. Write the beginning in such a way that it would immediately hook the reader. See the beginning of *1984* by George Orwell.

THE FIVE SENSES AND ONE-OF-A-KIND OBJECTS IN ONE-TIME EVENTS

EXERCISES:

○ Think of an unfamiliar sound in a familiar place. Focus on an object. Think of something you hear that you wish you hadn't heard. See what happened next. Catch the moment when there was a change from unpleasant to pleasant. Write in the present tense.

○ Think of unpleasant sensations in a beautiful place. Make a note of all the objects that come back to you. Put pluses and minuses next to each object. Choose the ones that have both a plus and a minus.

As soon as an inanimate object appears in our mind, we try to tell it as an oral telling. From start to finish we have a listener in mind. This is our rehearsal. We rehearse many times. Susan Cheever writes in the *New York Times Book Review,* how John Cheever would tell and retell events from his life. "Changing them, embroidering some anecdotes and shifting emphasis in others, adding sequences and even characters."[6]

---

6. September 9, 1984.

The best place to begin is among the tangibles of real life. Here is where you have authority. Author and authority go together. We know the material of our lives subjectively, but by focusing on objects we are moving into the objective and the universal. Objects in real life have a luminous quality on the page when they are seen through the lens of a powerful emotion. By themselves, the objects are no more interesting than a list of basic emotions, but when the object and the emotion become one, the reader's or listener's attention is immediately hooked. To sustain the intensity of the seeing, it is important that we catch short movements. These will later join hands to become longer pieces.

IN EACH INSTANCE, FEEL THE TENSION OF OPPOSITES

EXERCISES:

- We understand the importance of opposites. We want tension on the page. Every time there is a plus, we look for a minus and then we work in the contrast. If there is a person who sees Cousin Tim as *powerless*, we try to show him as *powerful*. In a story by William Carlos Williams, "The Use of Force,"[7] powerful adults are shown to be powerless and the child reduces the doctor to her own primitive level. Read the story and underline the objects in it.

- Get in touch with your five senses. Invite the material through your senses. Think of opposites: pleasant / unpleasant, happy / unhappy, victim / victimizer; then think of object, place, person, and event. Each time, put down a physical sensation. Do not stretch or pad, and do not explain. Set aside. These will work in your subconscious and later will open up into movements.

- Think of opposites, for example, heaven and hell. Think of a tangible you associate with heaven or hell, something you can touch, or taste, or smell, or see, or hear. A person may experience instinctual life as hell, or as heaven.

- Make a list of inanimate objects that come to your mind when you think of anger. Let these objects be from real life. Think of a time you saw someone who did not know (s)he was being observed, and note down the object that comes into your mind. What is the opposite event that comes into your mind when you think of this object? Tell us something that would hook us. Remember, you are a storyteller.

---

7. Irving Howe and Llana Wiener Howe, eds., *Short Shorts* (New York: Bantam, 1982), pp. 132-36.

In writing stories, we try to connect the familiar with the unfamiliar, the public with the less public, just as we do in metaphors. From the smallest unit of narration to the largest, this kind of yoking together extends the meaning of a story until it continues to expand in the mind of the reader. It's like yeast in dough, and we call this "the leavening principle."

EXERCISE:

- Think of: a familiar object in a strange place; a familiar person in a strange place; an odd thing that happened during a familiar ritual. Feel the emotion in each instance. Write down the sequence exactly as it enters your mind. Set aside for later use.

IMAGES OF FATHER:

- Think of all the words that come to your mind when you think of the word "father." Look over the list and find tangibles for each entry. Feel each object, and place pluses and minuses next to each entry. Set aside.

Most people have their mother's mythology, and fathers seem at first somewhat remote. There are exceptions, where the reverse is true, but as we progress in our writing, we discover deeper connections with the more remote of the two. Both men and women benefit from writing images of father. You may begin either with the most recent event or with the earliest, and work back and forth. Brainstorm for objects, places, persons, and problems you associate with father. Look for tangibles in each entry. Select the ones that have both a plus and minus. As an entry opens up, start taking down dictation from the way it enters your mind. Stop before the very end. Do not try to conclude or tie everything up in a neat knot. Reread what you have written and set it aside for later use. These short images can be donated to characters in your fiction.

It is best not to rewrite until you have written four or five hundred pages. Each time you do an exercise, you are learning something; what you learn will go into your next piece, and so on. In the beginning, you may think that you are writing simple entries. Nothing is simple; your simple piece is part of a complex whole that you will find only by writing a great deal. According to the method that we use in this manual, shorter pieces will join hands and become longer pieces, and each bit is a brick that will build the unparaphraseable whole. Do not be too analytical; do not approach this method as one would an academic project. What we need here is the ability to get in touch with an emotion that is a universal. It is this emotion that gives unity to the image. We don't know the full range of what we can do until we have done the first draft. Each time you write a true image, you discover something new, and the sense of wonder and discovery is what makes good fiction different from other kinds of prose writing.

EXERCISES:

- Make a list of all the father figures in your life and brainstorm for inanimate objects that you associate with each. Put pluses and minuses next to each object. Pick the ones that have both a plus and a minus. Remember that without conflict there is no story. See which of them will open up.

- Is there an object that brought you into conflict with someone who had the power to punish you? Focus on the object and place and person. Tell it rapidly. Listen to yourself and write down the sequence as it comes. Write the endings first; remove all modifiers.

- Write about an enjoyable event that was disapproved of by someone close to you.

"Everybody knows there is no fineness or accuracy in suppression; if you hold down one thing you hold down the adjoining."[8] It must follow that the opposite is also true. We have found in our workshops that the moment a participant releases one hidden object, dozens of others come to the surface. This process of surfacing more and more objects from the past starts the process toward greater creativity. The energy thus released spills into other areas of the participant's life, and we hear of participants surprising themselves and others by new levels of achievement in whatever they undertake. If you hold down one thing, you hold down the adjoining; if you liberate one image, you liberate the next.

EXERCISE:

- If we liberate one memory from where it is locked away, we liberate dozens of adjoining ones. Similarly, each basic emotion calls up dozens of new images.

    For example, list:

    - All the times that you have felt fear.
    - All the times you've seen fear in other people.
    - Fears that were reasonable and fears that were unreasonable.
    - Fears of a group, or race, or nation.

        Next to each entry, put down objects that come to your mind when you think of each instance when fear was a basic emotion. Some of these will open up to a sequence of what-happened-next.

Once we have done this, there is a momentum. Each object that is authentic will call up other objects. If you suppress one, you suppress dozens of others. If you free one object by opening it up, you liberate dozens of others. This has to be experienced to be believed.

---

8. Saul Bellow, *The Adventures of Augie March* (New York: Viking, 1953), p. 7.

WHY CHILDHOOD?

Our immediate past is not a useable past for creative writers. Of the material over which we have the most authority, places and people and events from childhood are the best for a first work of fiction. This is because we have already done the work of selecting and arranging. Writers and nonwriters alike mythify and legendize the events of childhood. We have gained distance and understanding. We can be both actor and chronicler about this period.

THE CHILD IS THE FATHER OF THE WRITER

The material from childhood affords the best opportunity for learning the use of dramatic irony. In writing about the child, we shouldn't be childish or childlike. There is the child and there is the grown person who is the narrator/writer; the distance between the two creates two levels of meaning, for there are the things that appeared to the child and there are those that only the grown person (author) knows. As far as the basic emotions are concerned, the child is the father of the writer—therefore, listen to the child. But the vocabulary or art with which we focus on the events of childhood, the way we listen to the sequence, these were not what the child would have told, had he done so then. The tension between the reality then and the manner of telling it now teaches us something valuable about the distance between author and character.

Object as Symbol

THE DRAMATIC USE OF OBJECTS

INANIMATE OBJECTS

EXERCISES:

- Make parallel columns: in one, put down objects you associate with characters in fiction, and in the other, objects you associate with persons in real life. To recognize the different uses of objects, think of the following examples: in the opening three pages of *Madame Bovary*, Flaubert uses a cap to characterize Charles Bovary and to set him apart from his classmates. Objects are sometimes used dramatically: the action of a play or story is built around an object, for example, the packet of Camels in James Thurber's story, "The Catbird Seat," in which the cigarettes are analogous to the murder weapon in a whodunit.

- Objects objectify. Without objects there would be no willing suspension of disbelief on the part of the reader. Objects create space on the page; without objects, there can be no scenes. Reread the opening pages of *Madame Bovary* and underline all the objects. Circle those that have a dramatic function.

When the several levels of meaning in a work of fiction get attached to an object, that object might be said to be symbolic. But this is a term that need not concern you. This word is more suitable for criticism. Writers who go symbolizing self-consciously are mostly fakers. The actual symbolizing is done by the subconscious, and the less the writer is aware of such "literary" terms, the better his work. One cannot interfere with the process in which objects enter our consciousness. This needs to be emphasized.

We will be hearing more about objects. Fiction is the art of moving outward, and the real tables and chairs create the space on the page.

SHORT SEGMENTS OF TIME
WHEN SOMETHING HAPPENED

EXERCISES:

- NARROW / BROAD   LOW / HIGH

  TIGHT / LOOSE   STRAIGHT / CROOKED

  Invite objects into your mind when you think of each of these opposites. Think of a one-of-a-kind tangible and then think of something that happened. Make quick notes.

- Think of the people in your life at the time of your earliest memory. Put down their names and place objects next to each name. Put pluses and minuses next to each object, according to pleasure or pain. In writing fiction we must be true to emotions and we must be faithful to objects. If we do this, there won't be anything fake on the page.

- Think of a time when you met someone who reminded you of a person who was in your earliest memory. Think of other persons who remind you of this person. Make a list and look for objects you associate with each person. See which of these will open up. Write the one that interests you most.

- Focus on an object; see the place, the person, and the event. Feel the event. Feel the beginning, middle, and end. Choose a short segment of time. *Write the ending.* Read the last three sentences of Hemingway's *A Farewell to Arms*, and compare your ending with his. Remove explanations and modifiers.

- Think of your first separation from a place or person. Think of a time when your family moved. Think of short images. Do not try to turn them into a preconceived mold. Just follow the way the objects surface. Open one entry in the present tense. Then translate it into the simple past.

- Choose one of these events and look for a one-of-a-kind object. Focus on place and person and event. Write the ending first. Reread the ending. See that there is no explanation, and see that there are no adjectives and adverbs.

HOW IT FEELS

It is the basic emotion that gives unity to an image. Point of view is related to where an emotion is coming from. We see what happens through the lens of how it feels. Depth of emotion and intensity of seeing give power to an image. To begin with, we just make lists and short notes. This way we give ourselves permission to feel more deeply and to see more fully. It is important, therefore, to touch base.

EXERCISE:

- Make a list of the basic emotions that you were familiar with in childhood. Then look for objects to focus on for each of those emotions. Next, put a plus and minus against each of those objects, and look for those that have both a plus and a minus. See which of these will open up to give you a sequence in which something changed from familiar to unfamiliar or vice versa.

JEALOUSY: A GRAND LITERARY EMOTION

EXERCISES:

- Make a list of objects which your mother possessed which you wanted for yourself. Or make a list of objects which you possess which your mother once desired. Feel the basic emotion each time. Look up in the dictionary the difference between "envy" and "jealousy."

- Make a list of all the triangle situations, beginning with mother/father/child, and go through the various periods in your life or in the life of someone you know very well and find such triangles.

- Jealousy in another person: focus on object-place-person-time-event. Do not explain. Write it as a scene in a play. There should be no sentences that sound like stage directions. Instead, focus on objects.

- ENVY / JEALOUSY. Make parallel lists of times when you've been envious or jealous. Find objects and notice the difference between envy and jealousy. Think about all the times you've been jealous. Note down places, persons, and events. Find objects for each occasion.

OBJECTS HUMANIZE THE TOTALLY EVIL OR THE ALTOGETHER GOOD PERSON

There are people in real life that one might hate, but in brainstorming we would find even in such characters much that is not hateful. It is only in this sense that writing may be said to be liberating. When we write, we see more and we feel more. It is a kind of voyage of discovery. We surprise ourselves in the way our dreams surprise us.

If you perceive someone as totally evil, the moment you begin to focus on objects you will find that the character is more human than you imagined. Try thinking of someone you thought of as totally good or totally evil. Make a list of all the objects you associate with this person. Then consult your emotions and put pluses and minuses next to each object. Circle those objects that have both a plus and a minus and start writing about what happened in a short segment of time. Remember, we don't want more than what happened in a short segment of time. Catch the moment of change. Go to the next object and do likewise, and so on till you have opened up all the objects you associate with this person. Set aside; your subconscious will work on it.

Do not try to be literary or precious or pretty in your writing. Focus on the tangibles. Please do not explain anything. Try telling it to somebody and ask them to repeat it back to you. A successful telling is unparaphraseable. It can't be told without the objects and without the sequence of the original. Organic form is nothing but the sequence in which an event surfaces in the mind.

THE THIRD ELEMENT IN FICTION

In stories that a reader can read and reread many times, there is a sort of subtle infusion, a leavening ingredient, which creates a third element, a mysterious something that arches over the event and provides a frame for the story. This third element is present even when it is not visible on the page: its presence influences the response to a story; it goes with the two-or-more-problems in a story; it alerts the reader to the multiple levels of meaning possible.

In real life, the third element is often missing, but in fiction, it provides a spiritual dimension. In order to make the third element a part of your understanding of what makes a story great, you must learn to take apart stories that have stood the test of time. In short, you must learn to read like a writer.

READING AS A WRITER

Read: "Hands" in *Winesburg, Ohio* by Sherwood Anderson.

- Notice that the surface time of the story is of short duration. How much time do you think has elapsed between the time when the berry pickers called out to Wing Biddlebaum and the last sentence of the story? Notice that the depth time is over twenty years: twenty years earlier, he had been driven out of a town in Pennsylvania, where he was a gifted teacher, to become an outcast in Winesburg, Ohio.

- If you were to divide the story into two parts, where would you make the division.

- If you were to further divide the first half, where would you make the division? Continue till you reach the first paragraph and finally the first sentence of the story.

- Go over Sentence One and see how each phrase relates to the rest of the paragraph as well as to the rest of the story. For example: "the half-decayed veranda," "the edge of a ravine near the town," and "the fat little old man" walking "nervously up and down" in the opening sentence suggest the movement of the rest of the story.

- Notice
  how the camera moves outside and creates the town with a minimum of words; how the sights and sounds in Paragraph One suggest the isolation of Wing Biddlebaum and his physical distance from life of the town; and how the opening sentence is echoed in the last sentence of the paragraph, and how this last sentence in its turn is echoed by the opening sentence of Paragraph Two. Notice the connection between the ghostly hair and the "ghostly band of doubts."

- Likewise, divide the second half of the story till you reach the last sentence of the final paragraph. Compare this final sentence with the beginning and notice how a new element has entered the story. This element, for want of a term, might be called the third element. In the ending, there is a religious or spiritual metaphor. This metaphor is not given to us through the character, but from the narrator. Wing Biddlebaum has just finished his meager supper, and as his fingers flash back and forth eating crumbs of bread, he seems to the narrator to be telling "decade after decade of his rosary." The rosary is a Christian symbol: Wing Biddlebaum is not necessarily a Christian. By casting over this moment the air of a religious rite of expiation, the author wakes the reader to the idea of a scapegoat who has taken upon himself the burden of the sin he was accused of, even though he is innocent. This suggestion is the third element.

EXERCISE:

- In the story "Hands," Sherwood Anderson concentrated on Wing Biddlebaum's hands. Make a list of persons who are important to you, but whom you no longer see. Think of one feature or gesture that comes back to you when you think of these people whom you once knew but who are no longer present. Set aside for donating later to fictional characters.

BLOODBANK

Think of the images on the clothesline as a banking system. We sometimes call it a bloodbank. We give transfusions to our characters. A little bit of our own experience ought to be shared with the least of our characters—villain and hero alike are part of the consortium. Shakespeare gave himself equally to Hamlet and Iago. Hamlet was on the side of the angels, and Iago, of the devils, but both are palpably human and Shakespearean.

In the clothesline school, for the first year, or during the first draft, we collect images with basic human emotions. We see to it that the subjectivity of the emotion appears on the page through an object. We attempt to make the private and the personal objective and accessible to the reader. The next step is to learn to share these images with other characters—to donate them to the characters we create.

OBJECT, PLACE, PERSON, AND EVENT — PART 2

LISTENING FOR STORIES: PLACES AND PEOPLE

Eudora Welty said, "Long before I wrote stories, I listened for stories. Listening for them is something more acute than listening to them." She went on to say, "I had to grow up and learn to listen for the unspoken as well as the spoken." The most important word here is *listening*. Listening, like charity, begins with oneself. How can we listen to others if we have never listened to ourselves? Most of us stopped listening to ourselves quite early. There is a storyteller in each of us, and we must learn to find entertainment in the way events enter and re-enter our minds. What entertains us is likely to entertain others. One way of finding our own voices is to take down dictation from the teller of tales inside us.

THE THIRD ELEMENT IN THE STORY

Without conflict, there is no story. The "pluses" on the page have to be earned. The moment one thinks of "love," for example, one remembers real-life events. Listen to the way these events surface in your mind, and you will find in each segment of time more than one problem, and a third element. For example, in the following poem by Stevie Smith, the third element is love, *in absentia*:

CORRESPONDENCE BETWEEN MR. HARRISON IN NEWCASTLE
AND MR. SHOLTO PEACH HARRISON IN HULL
Sholto Peach Harrison you are no son of mine
And do you think I bred you up to cross the River Tyne
And do you think I bred you up (and mother says the same)
And do you think I bred you up to live a life of shame
To live a life of shame my boy as you are thinking to
Down south in Kingston-upon-Hull a traveller in glue?
Come back my bonny boy nor break your father's heart
Come back and marry Lady Susan Smart
She has a mint in Anglo-Persian oil
And Sholto never more need think of toil

You are an old and evil man my father
I tell you frankly
Sholto had much rather
Travel in glue unrecompensed unwed
Than go to church with oily Sue and afterwards to bed.[1]

---

1. *The Oxford Book of Contemporary Verse 1945-1980*, D. J. Enright (Oxford University Press, 1980), p. 5. Reprinted by permission of New Directions Publishing Corporation.

HOLD THE MIRROR UP TO AN IMPERFECT WORLD

Fortunately for fiction writers, human love, like anything human, is imperfect. Sartre has given a persuasive explanation of why lovers inevitably suffer conflict and pain, but as fiction writers, we don't need such explanations. We need to attend to real situations; we actively look for conflict and then we catch a moment of change when something happened. Our approach is not analytical.

EXERCISES:

- Make parallel lists of beautiful and ugly places. Look for objects in each place. Put a plus or minus against each object. Mark the ones that have both a plus and a minus.

- A beautiful place where no one felt safe, and a time when you went there: re-enter the moment. Focus on an object. What happened next?

- A place and a season and a smell. Focus on an object. An activity that you associate with a festival or celebration. See who is doing what, in a one-time event that happened during a seasonal activity. Take down who said what. Look for a conflict, a problem, a mystery.

- Make parallel lists of safe and unsafe places. Look for objects in each place. Put a plus or minus against each object. Mark the ones that have both a plus and a minus.

- List childhood hideouts. Brainstorm for touch and taste and smell and sight and sound in these places. Do not stretch. It's enough if these are one-liners.

- Think of a place where you spent a lot of time as a child. Make two columns, one for objects that have changed, and another for objects that have not changed. Read Hawthorne's "Roger Malvin's Burial" and find the one object that changed the most.

- A place where you felt excited. List all the times you felt both excited and afraid. Look for objects. Think of a person you associate with one of these places.

- A narrow place where you felt free. Focus on a sensation. See an object. Look for a prior problem. Do not begin with the prior problem. Let it come out after you have entered into what happened next.

- A forbidden place where you were always welcome. Focus on an object. See the person. See what happened next. Do not explain.

- A dark place where something good happened. What's the prior problem? Feel the plus and the minus. Feel the emotion. Follow the sequence.

- A place that doesn't exist anymore. Focus on an object and tell what comes into your mind. Write rapidly the sequence in which the event surfaces.

- A place that hasn't changed, and a person who has changed beyond recognition. Focus on an object. Feel the emotion. Write the ending without explanations. Use no adjectives or adverbs.

- Think of a neighborhood or small town you know well. Think of events or situations that lifted barriers and brought people together. These could be local, national, or international. Learn to consult old newspapers in libraries.

- Make a list of people you have disliked. Avoid evaluations; just move the camera, and let the camera record what it can, and let the reader be the judge. Do not interfere with the reader's ability to judge for himself or herself.

- A segment of time and a place where you felt let down; focus on an object which you disliked. Choose a short segment of time. Get in touch with your five senses. Feel the emotion. Without conflict, there is no story.

- A place and a public event that united everybody. See one person who did not participate. Choose a short segment of time when someting happened. What did this person say?

- A place and an activity that brought on conflict. Feel the conflict. Write in the present tense. Record direct speech where possible. Consult your favorite book or story on how to enter dialogue.

- A place that keeps changing. List objects that have not changed. See which of these objects have a dramatic function in what happened next. Follow the object. Take down dictation as thing follows thing.

- A place you liked made imperfect by the presence of a person you disliked. Do not explain. Tell what happened.

- Think of a place where someone felt free. Look at a prior problem. Brainstorm for object, place, person, and event. Choose a short segment of time. Tell it in the present tense.

- Think of a place where someone felt trapped. Focus on an object. See who else is present. Hear what is said. Tell it in the present tense.

PLACES

In each telling, think of: Object, Time, Place, Event, Person. Wherever you lived, was there:

- A place where people came together?
- A place where they came together in conflict?
- If you lived in two places, was there someone who shared both places with you?
- Was there a town gossip?
- Was there a person that most people disliked? A person everybody liked?
- Did somebody have to leave town?
- Did a stranger come?
- Was there a special place?
- Was someone very rich? Or very poor?
- Was there a do-gooder?
- Was there someone whose bark was worse than his/her bite?
- Was there anyone crazy?
- Was there a very strange family?
- Was there a secret that everyone knew?
- Was someone very religious?
- Was there a most evil person in town?
- Was there ever a miracle?
- Was there work most people participated in?
- Did people change with the seasons?
- Were young people replicas of the older generation?
- Was there any woman in town other women didn't like? Or a man?
- Did anybody die in town?
- Did anybody take a risk?
- Was the whole town ever afraid?
- Was there anyone that the neighborhood would listen to?

HAVE YOU READ "THE BLUE HOTEL" BY STEPHEN CRANE?

EXERCISE:

- Think of the word "danger."

    Make two columns, one for physical danger and the other for mental.

    Find objects in each case. Underline those that will open up for later use.

    Translate abstract words into concrete things.

A DRAMATIC OBJECT: THE HANDKERCHIEF IN *OTHELLO*

Shakespeare's use of the handkerchief in *Othello* is an example of how an object can have a dramatic function in a play or novel. In the play, Othello gives two different versions of why the handkerchief is important to him. In the second version,[2] he tells us that it was given to his mother by an Egyptian who could read the thoughts of people; she told his mother that as long as she owned the handkerchief it would make her "amiable" and would "subdue" her husband, but should she lose it or give it away, her husband would find her "loathed" and he would "hunt after new fancies." Dying, the mother gave Othello the handkerchief and asked him to give it to his future wife. Othello's mother had no confidence in the constancy of love, and the manner in which the handkerchief is handed down supposes that Othello does not either.

As far as his "script" is concerned, this is not all. Desdemona has brought to her marriage her only story from before she met Othello. Desdemona's mother had a maid called Barbara. She was in love, but he whom she loved proved mad. Barbara, the maid, died singing a song, and Desdemona begins to sing the song her mother's maid sang, as she sat by the sycamore tree, "her hand on her bosom, her head on her knee." This inset, given to us in IV, ii, 26-57, is both ironic and prophetic. The maid Barbara's "salt tears fell from her and softened the stones." Shakespeare uses the image of the stones from the point of view of Desdemona, who doesn't know she will be murdered by Othello who has been temporarily driven insane by jealousy due to the machinations of Iago. The stones might be softened, but not her husband.

2. III, iv, 55-63.

THE THREE UNITIES

In Aristotelian poetics, we have the unity of time, place, and action. Of the three, the unity of action is the most important. In our program, what gives unity to a short movement is the emotion. It is the emotion that relates the parts to the whole and makes it mean something to the listener.

What the central idea is to an essay, what the topic sentence is to a paragraph, the basic emotion is to a short movement in fiction. By emotion, we mean basic emotions people everywhere feel, that which is common to all men and women everywhere.

EXERCISE:

- List a few basic emotions: fear, anger, jealousy, hatred, frustration, and so on, and see how many of them were recurring emotions in your childhood. Once you have found your range of emotions, then you can go up and down the material at hand and find places and times when you felt them. Once you have located short segments of time for each instance, enter one of them by feeling the event as if it were happening again. As you re-enter, your eyes will fall on something tangible; start with that object. Do not explain. Plunge in, in the middle of the action. *Do not name the emotion*. If you do, the reader has no work.

A CASE OF BLOCKED EMOTIONS

If, when you are brainstorming, the same emotion turns up, do not worry. Clogged, clotted, congested, toxic emotions will leave us, as we begin to write. If a single event keeps coming up, if a single emotion (e.g., helplessness) keeps turning up every way you turn, here's what you may do: take the central event that recurs, and look around and see if you can find another person, or even an animal, in the same situation. Write about that event, and see what happened next. Feel for the animal or person, but see both the plus and the minus. Keep doing this for a while, and reread what you have written. Do not rewrite. Write rapidly as if taking down dictation from the voice inside. It is important that you focus on an object and write in the present tense. Do not attempt this exercise except in the present tense. This removes the clutter. Do not directly name the emotion.

Each time you liberate one image, dozens will get liberated of their own accord. If you suppress one, dozens go under. There may be an image you don't want anyone to see. Write it, tear it up, and trash it. The writing and rereading will have magical results. You will feel as if what you wrote filled you up in a new way. There will be pain when you write, but it is the kind of pain that is creative and it will add up to pleasure. The pain will disappear the moment you reread what you have written. The subjectivity will give way to the objectivity of contemplating something on a page.

THINKING IN TANGIBLES

Do not think in terms of "faith, hope, and charity." Think of one-of-a-kind objects, persons, places, and events. And think of their opposites. Think of the opposite of "church." If your answer is "state," watch out. It means you are running along the beaten path. The moment you think of "church," think of a one-time event. For example, think of the time Jessy was being baptized and she almost drowned. Think of the opposite movement in Jessy's life.

In good writing, the density on the page is derived from this sort of brainstorming. The tension of opposites gives energy to the page. Apart from this, this exercise has a beneficial effect. We go through life saying the same things about ourselves. We have clutched at a certain explanation which we continue to produce readily at the slightest enquiry into our affairs. Thinking of opposites will get us off the familiar grooves. We may be able to make some exciting discoveries. As writers, we keep ourselves open to these opposites. We invite these new movements. It is a free act of contemplation, and there is no harm in it. Unlike real life, the life on the page rewards you immediately; writing is in itself a rewarding and exciting activity. Our program is designed to make writing fiction a natural activity, like walking or running. Even when you are writing in your head and haven't yet put pen to paper, each time you rehearse a story, you experience the pleasure of heightened awareness.

THE TENSION OF OPPOSITES: HAPPINESS HAS TO BE EARNED ON THE PAGE

EXERCISES:

- ○ Supposing the emotion is love, think of the opposite of love: think of jealousy or indifference. Or, if you have the word "generous," think of its opposite: "ungenerous." Think of a moment when someone you loved was ungenerous. Look for an object. See what happened next. Write in the present tense. Read over and remove all adjectives and adverbs and explanations.

TOUCH	TASTE	SMELL	SIGHT	SOUND
		OBJECT		
	PLACE — PERSON — EVENT			
	SHORT UNITS OF TIME			

FIND OBJECTS FOR ANY OF THE FOLLOWING MOVEMENTS:

- FAMILIAR / UNFAMILIAR

- HAPPY / UNHAPPY

- INNOCENCE / EXPERIENCE

- PASSIVE / ACTIVE

- FAITH / DOUBT

- VICTIM / VICTOR

BASIC PATTERNS

We listen to ourselves creatively. We not only listen to what-follows-what, we begin to notice basic patterns. For example, do our movements go from happiness to unhappiness, innocence to experience, familiar to unfamiliar, or vice versa? Are we alternating between active and passive, between faith and doubt, between being victim or being victor, and so on? Write five lines, ten lines, a page. Do not pad. Do not stretch. Write lean. Less is more.

Think in short movements. Do not try to build more than one arch. Each time, feel the emotion. Focus on one thing that anyone can touch, taste, smell, see, hear. We want to focus on an image that will suggest to the reader how it feels to be in a particular situation. The "how it feels" gives unity to the telling.

- The "how it feels" cannot be faked.

- The object must be from real life.

Be patient. Rome wasn't built in a day and, as Freud points out, there is the Roma Quadrata and the Aurelian city and the Servian city, and all the past cities still visible in the present city of Rome, and so also in "mental life," nothing which has once been formed can perish.[3] Everything adds up and will fall into place, box within box. Nothing is simple, neither the parts nor the whole. These images are not "simple." Example: Jillian saves bib lettuce for her friend, "Penny My Duck," in a dinner napkin on her lap. The family takes turns looking after "Penny My Duck" whenever Jillian is away at school. She helps herself to chicken, bolts her dinner, and runs out with the stolen lettuce, only to discover that the "chicken" she ate was the much-adored "Penny My Duck." There is a connection between this image and fifty others, but we do not analyze or explain. Let the reader do the explaining. *Do not pad; do not stretch. Catch a moment of change.*

EXERCISE:

○ Find tangibles for the following opposites:

WHITE / BLACK	SWEET / BITTER
SMOOTH / ROUGH	MILD / SHARP
STEADY / INTERMITTENT	

In each instance, feel the emotion. We want one-of-a-kind objects. Alternate between indoors and outdoors. Be aware of space. Be aware of a short segment of time. Be particularly aware of emotion in each instance. Make a note. This part of the brainstorming is intense and wordless. Sit down in a comfortable position and feel / touch / taste / smell / see / hear. Keep back the words for as long as you can. One of the above might be clamoring to be written. Write down rapidly what comes into your mind. Set aside for later use.

RAPID WRITING

SWEET / SOUR	SMELLS		PLACE
HARD / SOFT	SIGHT		
SOLID / LIQUID	SOUND	OBJECT	PERSON
GRAINY / SMOOTH	TASTE		EVENT
LOVING / UNLOVING	TOUCH		

---

3. Sigmund Freud, *Civilization and Its Discontents* (New York: W.W. Norton & Co., Inc., 1961), p. 16.

EXERCISES:

- The first time you fell in love. Focus on an object. Think of two problems, and a third element. Focus on an inanimate object.

- A moment that changed from innocence to experience for you or for someone else. Focus on an object, a place, a person, and the event. This exercise will yield different stories at different sessions. A recurring movement of this kind should be attempted more than once.

Brainstorm for place, person, event in such a way that the reader gets hooked and wants to know what happened next.

HOT / COLD	
SMOOTH / GRAINY	
SHARP / MILD	OBJECT
UP / DOWN	
LOUD / SOFT	

You may make up such exercises every day, the way musicians practice scales. Write rapidly, exactly as it enters your head; if you tamper with the sequence, you will have prose, but not fiction.

BEGINNINGS: HOOKING THE READER

Practice writing the beginning of a movement. Each time you begin, it is most probably a false beginning which tries to explain or describe a setting. None of this is needed. For the reader, there ought to be the excitement of discovering something, of making connections, of linking two separate things from different parts of the story. In order to make this possible, enter the event in the middle of the action. Usually, if you cannot find a focus in the beginning, it will become focused after you have written a bit. Rehearsing in the head is a good idea, but at the same time, make notes, for it might vanish as your dreams vanish; you may never be able to enter the sequence in quite the same brilliant way. I am not using the word "brilliant" carelessly. When a person really listens to an event, and hears the sequence, and takes down dictation, it is usually better than what passes for good writing. After you have finished the ending, go back and write a different beginning.

Fiction writers must learn to move the camera outward. Focus on objects. See what happened next. Do not settle inside the mind of a narrator or a character. The mind is a narrow place, and since some of us have claustrophobia, please spare us: move the camera outward. The objects in the place give objectivity to your story. Without the objects, there is no space for the reader. Learn to write lean.

EXERCISES:

- Think of a moment when you or someone else felt jealous. Focus on an object. Tell it in the present tense. Go over the beginning. See if you have a false beginning.

- A time when you were attracted to someone unsuitable, or, a suitable person whom you found to be unattractive. Look for an object. Do not start with "When I was . . . ." This is a confessional, or autobiographical mode. Focus by moving outward.

- Find an event when you meant to do something bad, but it turned out good, or vice versa. Focus on an object, think of the place, the person(s), the event; choose a short segment of time. Do not explain anything. Try it in the present tense which helps remove clutter and teaches you to follow the sequence. Translate back to the simple past, which is the narrative tense.

- Think of something horrible that happened to someone you liked. See how it changed your relationship. Focus on an object. Choose short segments of time.

FICTION

Fiction is different from a newspaper story. The main difference is that there is a relation between the beginning, the middle, and the end in fiction. Usually there is more than one level of meaning, and any part of a good story would have the strengths of the whole.

The fiction writer writes in such a way that the reader has a sense of what is to come, even though the characters in the story do not. The fiction writer creates space and distance within the story. There is distance between author and character, even though the writer may have donated experiences from his own life to the characters.

PEOPLE

WARM-UP EXERCISES:

- Sensations. Opposites. Suggest tangibles for the following opposites:

OPEN / CLOSED	IN / OUT
UP / DOWN	NARROW / WIDE
STRAIGHT / CROOKED	EARLY / LATE
MORNING / EVENING	NOON / MIDNIGHT
WEEKDAY / WEEKEND	

- Think of opposites in your dreams. Tell a dream that has something to do with a real place.

- Put the name of a person next to each of the following adjectives. If you know a generous person, put his or her name down, and then think of someone miserly. Put down more opposite types.

SILENT / TALKATIVE	HONEST / DISHONEST
RELIABLE / UNRELIABLE	

  Continue thinking of persons till you reach someone about whom you have something to tell. Focus on something tangible, and tell rapidly what comes into your mind. Do not explain; do not pad; do not try to stretch it into a story. Take a person who is a type and free him from the type by thinking of a one-time event. Focus on an object that is one-of-a-kind.

BUILDING A PERSON: BRAINSTORMING EXERCISES:

- Choose a person you love or hate—someone you know as well as can be expected. List objects you connect with this person. Focus on one object at a time, and write about it on a card; set it aside. Do this with as many objects as you can use. *Remember—you are a storyteller.*

- The person and a gesture.

- The person and a phrase or sentence.

- Something that happened to this person when he/she was little.

- A dream this person had.

- A time this person lost something or found something.

- A time when the person triumphed over odds.

- Someone who had power over this person.

- Something the person destroyed.

- Imagine a group of people in a room and put this person in their midst; a bit of conversation: learn to give an illusion of several persons talking without too much dialogue.

- An old problem this person had.

- A time when this person felt, "I did not like what I did."

- Should have felt the above and didn't.

- When the person cried for no reason, or for a reason.

- Unconscious act of cruelty.

- A conscious act of cruelty.

- This person in the street; when alone.

- A lie this person told.

- A characteristic trait, an uncharacteristic act.

- Where this person felt most comfortable, least comfortable.

- When you least/most liked this person.
  Reread and remove all adjectives and adverbs wherever possible.
  Do not name the basic emotion directly.

MORE PERSON EXERCISES:

- An absurd situation created by this person.

- Someone this person competed with.

- A conversation about this person you overheard.

- A monologue by this person.

- What was the most important event in this person's life?

- His or her earliest memory.

- Something this person didn't know about, that would make a difference if he/she knew.

You can continue with this and make up more exercises. They may be used when brainstorming for characters. Enter some of these on cards and file them. Have an easy retrieval system so that you can donate an item from one life to fill a spot in another. *Most of the characters in fiction are composites*. In each segment of time, think of object, place, person, event, and segment of time. It is not worth recording if, in the short segment of time, something did not change. There may be a movement from unhappiness to happiness, from familiar to unfamiliar, from innocence to experience, faith to doubt, and so on. Each image has its own movements.

POINT OF VIEW

Point of view is related to the basic emotion. It is also a tool in projecting, focusing, and moving from one moment in time to the next. We're all locked into our own persons. As Anatole France said, "If only we could see through the eyes of a donkey or a fly." Writing, the act of creation, makes us able to do just that, see through the eyes of donkeys or flies.

MAINSTREAM IMAGES

Even though the finished piece of writing (short image or novel) might seem experimental, the shorter units within the piece, the units we took off the clothesline to form the larger piece, will each have the traditional unities. We haven't gotten too far away from classical notions of form in the basic building blocks of fiction. This is because form is intrinsic to the way we see things. Without form, communication is not possible. Notice how a well-made sentence has "plot" in the traditional sense.

This is more visible on the stage: the unities may not be strictly maintained within a play as a whole, but within each segment of the action they are essential.

In fiction, surface time is what gives structure to the short movements. We enter this segment of time by focusing on something outside our own selves, something that others can touch or taste or smell or see or hear. As we begin to re-enter an event, our attention will fall on something that is tangible; focus on that and tell what happened next.

Most people find it hard to focus on tangibles even though at night their dreams have brilliant objects. There are ways of learning to see the world through the senses by trying simple exercises each day. Begin by making a note of inanimate objects in your dreams. Then underline objects in the classics you read. For example, open *Madame Bovary* and start marking objects. Underline those objects that have a special function with a different colored ink.

In a picaresque novel, the rogue-hero travels from place to place. Each event occurs in a different place and is held together because it happened to one person. This gives us a kind of horizontal movement. Since the days of the picaresque novel in the eighteenth century, we have become aware of another kind of movement, which is vertical.

James Joyce is the great master of vertical movement. In his writing, objects achieve a luminous quality, for example, the chalice in "The Sisters." We see the chalice empty, broken, and buried, and the object suggests the physical, the emotional, and the spiritual condition of these Dubliners.

"The Sisters" alternates between direct and indirect narration. We hear and see as in a play the passages in direct speech which the boy overhears: (a) what the men believed, and (b) what the women believed. This is given to us objectively, as in a well-made play. The unities of time and place and the unity of emotion are strictly maintained. In the indirect narrative that frames the direct speech, the narrator takes different units of time, memories of events, and weaves them around three key words: *paralysis, gnomon, simony*—one from the spiritual world, another from the material world, and a third from the intellectual world. Joyce makes them arch over the narrative so that they color the story.

VERTICAL AND HORIZONTAL MOVEMENTS

Saul Bellow, who has absorbed the Joycean notion of epiphanies, what Joyce calls "the soul of the commonest object," the sudden illumination that comes to us in moments of heightened perception, is a master of the vertical view. He has two kinds of vertical movements: (1) the kind that leaps out of common objects in space, and (2) the kind that comes to him in what he calls "a levitation toward the truth," which has to do with putting units of time together.

Here's an example of what Joyce calls a "sudden spiritual manifestation" through a common object. At a moment when his patron is dying, a survivor of the holocaust sees

> a vacant building opposite marked for demolition. Large white X's on the windowpanes. On the plate glass of the empty shop were strange figures or non-figures in thick white. Most scrawls could be ignored. These for some reason caught on with Mr. Sammler as pertinent. Eloquent. Of what? Of future nonbeing.[4]

The X's remind him of death because his patron is dying. Two dissimilar things are being brought together. In this sense, our best images are metaphors. The image is not contrived; it appears on the page from really listening. Death or demolition can be a powerful leit-motif. Elsewhere, Mr. Bellow writes, "The sun shone brightly as if there were no death." The use of the subjunctive here makes the sudden point of illumination connect up with several other pluses and minuses.

AFFINITIES AND CONTRASTS

Time is measured in intervals. Two units of time from different periods in a person's life can be placed, one near the other, as if in the same afternoon, as contiguous. The reader connects the two and sees affinities and contrasts, so that the two units of time are welded together to make an image, or movement. Where possible, avoid the use of words like "today" or "now" or "yesterday" to denote the time; this breaks the illusion for the reader. You may use these words denoting time if your narrative is in the form of a "diary" or "journal," as in the *Horla* by Maupassant. Read each page of fiction carefully many times, till you have learned all that you can from each page. Reading like a writer is quite different from reading for entertainment.

Do not try to write long and complicated epics in one sitting! Choose short segments of time. Remind yourself to do this. The purity of listening, the power of the emotion, the ability of the senses to make visible on the page that which is not visible, all this is possible if you stop as soon as you have caught a moment of change. Don't be wordy. When you have done hundreds of such short units, longer ones will form out of these shorter units. The process of how this happens is mysterious and cannot be described. You have to discover this for yourself.

4. Saul Bellow, *Mr. Sammler's Planet* (New York: Viking, 1970), p. 93.

PERSONS: NEITHER TOO GOOD NOR TOO EVIL

Aristotle was right: the totally evil and the totally good are not visible on the page. Participants in our workshops arrive thinking of X or Y as totally bad or unredeemable or hateful. But in brainstorming for objects belonging to such characters, they find each character's common humanity, their pluses as well as their minuses.

Another thing that frequently happens is a change in the hierarchy of the interesting, more interesting, and most interesting characters. The moment one puts down one object, several others clamor to be put down. The hidden life within us has a different hierarchy from that of the conscious lives we lead. Participants arrive at the workshop thinking that a particular parent was more important than the other and end up writing powerful images about the parent they thought was not important.

Fiction is derived from epic, romance, drama, folk tale, journalism, biography, travelogue, etc. But in its most dramatic form, it owes most to the well-made play. In our writing, the camera eye of the narrator moves outward as in a film, focusing on place and time and event. In our writing, the unity of action comes from the unity of feeling, but we never directly tackle the feeling, we look for the *"objective correlative"* of the feeling by really listening to what we saw, what we heard, what we touched, smelled, or tasted. If we do this, our creativity is released, and we enter a new realm which comes from the same source that dreams come from.

IF YOU SUPPRESS ONE IMAGE, DOZENS OF IMAGES WILL BE LOST; IF YOU LIBERATE ONE MEMORY, DOZENS WILL SURFACE IMMEDIATELY.

Writing is a discovery of a hidden power, and it's so simple. For example, most participants think that they don't have dreams or that their dreams are not interesting. We tell them to bring us one or two objects from a dream and to keep a notebook at their bedside. In no time, they come back inundated with objects and records of dreams. Creative writing works in the same way. Each object we put down releases dozens of other objects.

By now, as a result of having worked through a hundred-odd images, we have learned to write without explanations. We have been in touch with our feelings. We have learned to recognize incidents in real life, to respect our own voice and perceptions, and we have learned to listen to ourselves and to other people.

STRUCTURE

PART 3

AT THE HEART OF EVERY GOOD IMAGE IS A MYSTERY, SOMETHING UNPARAPHRASEABLE

"Paper Pills" by Sherwood Anderson contains twelve paragraphs; paragraphs eight and nine contain a puzzle and a mystery. The key to the puzzle is the girl's dream that one of her suitors had bitten into her body and that his jaws were dripping blood. In actual fact, the man talked about virginity. She had the dream three times. She assumes that he is filled with a greater lust than the others. She gets impregnated by another man who said not a word, but who, in a moment of passion, actually bit her. She goes to Dr. Reefy, and Anderson uses a euphemism to say that she had an abortion. She marries Dr. Reefy, an older man, whose knuckles looked like "clusters of unpainted wooden balls as large as walnuts, fastened together by steel rods."

There is a central mystery here that we have to figure out. The storyteller wakes us up by not explaining. The dark girl dies soon afterwards. Perhaps Dr. Reefy inherits her wealth. She's the only one he shared his thoughts with. Of all the people of Winesburg, how did she qualify for this singular honor? What is the girl's sexual muddle? Can we blame the young man for her dreams? These questions continue in our minds after we've read the story. This is because Anderson leaves the image open. He doesn't try to tie everything up, or explain the why or wherefore. Yet, on re-examining it, we notice that there is only one sentence that is in direct speech in the whole story. Notice two objects in the story: the *window* and the *twisted apples.*

PRIOR PROBLEM AND COMPLICATION

Although stories have beginnings and ends, just as in real life, in fiction, too, every event has a prior problem, a complication that makes the event more complex. At the simplest level, the prior problem is related to the idea of contrast: the tension between opposites that gives new energy to the life on the page. For example, a person who is living in a luxurious penthouse might have grown up in a basement apartment where all he or she could see out the window was the footwear of passersby. A person with no descendents might have been the eldest of nine children. A person who saved many lives might in the end be left alone to die, to be buried with no mourners.

However short the image we are writing, there is an idea or theme at the back of it. This is never to be explicitly stated. It is something the reader deduces from the difference between the beginning, the middle, and the end. As we begin to tell about the event, we have a vague notion of how it is to end. We often go back after we have finished and look at the beginning, to see whether we have managed a subtle infusion into the beginning of the way it is to end.

SENSATIONS - OBJECT - PERSON - EVENT - SEGMENT OF TIME

EXERCISES:

○ Make a list of all the times when you were happy, and then look for two problems in each instance. See what happened next.

○ Think of an act of revenge. Focus on an object.

ELIMINATE FALSE BEGINNINGS

Chances are, every image you write will have a false beginning: an elaborate setting-up of a scene, explaining the prior problem, description for its own sake, wordiness, or using objects that have really no true function. But suddenly the actual story begins; our voice becomes authentic; a real event is being engendered. Thing follows thing in an unquestionable sequence. We must go back and strike out the false beginning. And we must learn not to begin with the prior problem. Let the prior problem be embedded in the narrative, as in James Thurber's "The Catbird Seat."[1]

Most participants have their own notions of what a story ought to be. In the beginning of our program some feel that what they're writing are lists of objects, persons, events, and the longer pieces seem to them to be "simple little images." After a while, they discover that the movements are neither simple nor little, but that they're complex. They begin to notice connections between various units, and they begin to understand that the items on the clothesline are the basic building blocks of fiction. There's one question that persists at this point; they ask, "How can we create a plot?" There's no better story for studying plot than James Thurber's "The Catbird Seat."

---

1. *50 Great Short Stories*, Milton Crane, ed. (New York: Bantam, 1983), pp. 322-30.

A SEE-SAW STRUCTURE: STORY AND PLOT

Before we begin with "The Catbird Seat," it's good to refresh ourselves by looking up the seventh chapter of Aristotle's *Poetics*, since our notions of plot originate there. Thurber has taken the Aristotelian structure and made fun of it in "The Catbird Seat." At the same time, the unities of time and place and action, the beginning, middle, and end, climax, catastrophe, recognition, and reversal, have all been carefully worked out within the structure of the story.

The structure is what we earlier called a "see-saw structure." This is used to advantage when the theme is one of revenge. In this story, Mrs. Barrow is in the catbird seat at the beginning of the story, but Mr. Martin unseats her in the end. The first thing we notice in reading "The Catbird Seat" is that Thurber has structured the different layers of time. The surface time of the story, or the duration of time (from the time Mr. Martin bought his packet of cigarettes on Monday night to Mrs. Barrow being carried out on Wednesday), is two days. The prior problem has existed for a little less than two years, and the depth time is twenty years. The twenty years Mr. Martin has worked in this firm have established him as someone unfailingly trustworthy, and that turns out to be his alibi.

As usual, we should begin to read the story by marking all the objects. The object that opens the story is a pack of Camels. Paragraph One focuses on this object. The pack of Camels is comparable to the murder weapon in a detective story. Sentence One and Sentence Two of the story emphasize the time and the day when he bought it. The remaining three sentences are preoccupied with the furtive manner in which he bought it. The very last sentence of the paragraph is a very short one that says, "No one saw him." We are hooked by the mystery of why a man would buy a packet of cigarettes in this secretive manner, but the sentence before that foreshadows the rest of the plot. The narrator tells us that the people he worked with would have been surprised because Mr. Martin did not smoke and had never smoked.

The next paragraph advances the plot by telling us that Mr. Martin had decided to "rub out" Mrs. Barrows; a plus and a minus is given to us. The plus is Mr. Martin's past, and the minus is what he's about to do. We're also told that this plan of action had been hatched during seven days, beginning November 2, 1942. The precision with which these dates are used and the time scale add to our sense of the truth of Mr. Martin's case against Mrs. Barrows.

A METAPHOR

The next four paragraphs use the metaphor of an actual court case against Mrs. Barrows. The movement ends with the gavel coming down to demand the death penalty for Mrs. Barrows. The comedy of the situation is underlined by snippets of dialogue uttered by Mrs. Barrows, and the comparisons and descriptions reduce her further to the level of a horse, or a donkey, or a duck. The bits of dialogue put into the mouths of office assistants support Mr. Martin's case. Mr. Martin drinks milk during this movement and we find out that he has a head for dates. After all, he is the perfect cog in the official wheel, in charge of the filing department. This metaphor of a trial is a clever expository device to explain the prior problem.

REVERSAL AND RECOGNITION

The next movement begins on Tuesday. This is the day when the plot reaches its climax. At 9:00 P.M. he turns up at Mrs. Barrows' house. This section of the story is told in three distinct movements: the approach to Mrs. Barrows', the arrival at her place, and the execution of his plan. The first movement of the story is a perfect Aristotelian development. The "recognition" and the "reversal" coincide; Mrs. Barrows knows that Mr. Martin has tricked her. She exclaims, "My God it's really too perfect." She's carried out screaming and braying while Mr. Martin is sitting pretty in the catbird seat. The metaphor in the title catches the movement of the plot.

DIALOGUE

EXERCISES:

- Practice dialogue between two persons you know well. Hoda's husband wears the same scarf every winter and Hoda wants him to put it in the garbage bin. He refuses. Hoda has found out that the scarf was given to him as a parting gift by his ex-fiancee. Write a dialogue between the two. Be selective. Give the illusion of complete speech but do not reproduce every word a person may have uttered. Focus on the object and feel the emotion.

In using dialogue in a scene of conflict, remember that each character has his or her own script or scenario which is different from that of the others. This individuality should be maintained or it will sound like a debate or an argument. Hoda's husband may be trying to assert his independence, but Hoda's mind is haunted by the picture of her mother wearing a large sun hat, sitting on a beach, forever alone. The sequence does not have to be logical or rational, but it must be true emotionally.

We become aware of the uses of dialogue. When there is a head-on conflict between two characters, a scene in fiction is closest to a well-made play. At other times, a phrase or a direct quote, a snippet of conversation, can give an illusion of dialogue, as if we are in the presence of a speaker even though we are only giving significant phrases.

We cannot use in a story all the direct speech a character might use in real life. We select, keeping in mind that we are storytellers. We don't generally use dialogue to advance the storyline. There are more economical ways of doing that. We have already noticed how Joyce alternates between direct and indirect speech in "The Sisters." He does this to show the difference in the attitudes of the men and the women and he shows the boy narrator caught in the middle, listening silently. They punch contrasting impressions on the boy, who is somewhat damaged by these opposing forces. What is the third element? And this wakes us up to their situation, as well as to ours.

EXERCISES:

- Think of something you heard that you did not understand at the time.

- Hear a quarrel between two persons which reveals something that keeps coming back to you. Note down the sequence exactly as it enters your mind.

- Snatches of song and places where you heard them. Is there a song you associate with a member of your family? Choose a short segment of time in which something important happened to this person which changed the situation for better or worse.

- Think of a person. Put down phrases and favorite sayings of this person and something that this person said that you never understood. Focus on a moment when it began to make sense to you and tell it.

- Think of a person who said very little. Find objects you associated with this person. Put down what other people have said about this person. See this person at his/her best/worst.

- A person who loved cruel words and didn't know how to respond to kind words.

- Several persons in a room talking about an absent person whom no one understood.

- Several persons in a room talking about a common prejudice.

MONOLOGUES

Read Robert Browning's poem "My Last Duchess." The poem opens and closes with an object. Both tell us a great deal about the speaker. There are four persons involved in this piece: (A) the author; (B) the speaker; (C) the listener, who in this case is an emissary from the father-in-law-to-be; and (D) the reader (you). A is a very clever chap: he uses dramatic irony which distances him from the speaker. B, the speaker, has done something terrible, but he is in the grip of an emotion that we know to be a basic human emotion. He has the power and position to do something criminal (Seen the movie *Chinatown*?) and get away with it. He wakes us up, because we feel sympathetic (to envy or jealousy?), but at the same time we are forced to judge him. C, the listener, is a flunky, a factotum; he is perhaps not free to express his opinion of the speaker, but we know he is listening—the speaker is not distracted by him. Think of a head-of-state saying to an ally, "I gave commands; Then all smiles stopped together." (This line changes the meaning of the poem for us). Now look at the beginning and the ending. How do the last three lines of the poem affect our reading of the poem?

DRAMATIC MONOLOGUES:
EXERCISES:

- By a person who has been blamed for something.

- By a person who thinks the world is out to get him.

- By an irrational person who keeps reiterating that he or she is rational.

- By a person who is obsessed. For example, see James Joyce's "An Encounter" in *Dubliners*.

- By someone who has a problem about the listener.

READING LIKE A WRITER

Read "An Encounter" by James Joyce in *Dubliners*. Notice how the obsessions of the stranger are communicated in such a way that one feels one can hear him even though they are given to us in indirect speech. What is the difference between the attitude of the narrator in the beginning and at the end? What is the revelation? When writing your own, it does not matter if the entry is short. Do not stretch or try to make it into a story. Just follow the sequence as it enters your mind.

EXERCISE:

- The first stranger you met by yourself. Feel the basic emotion.

BLOOD TRANSFUSIONS

We are donating to our characters our energy. We have to find that energy within ourselves. In order to do so, we have to be aware of a certain force within us. We are at the center. We are related to everything. There is nobody bigger than us when it comes to seeing, touching, hearing, tasting, smelling. A few people in our lives may have interfered and come between us and our sensations. Forgive them. The moment you forgive them, your sensations will be restored in full measure. It's a very small adjustment in the brain. The creative part of you is large. It is what Walt Whitman called "Kosmos," and it is a very powerful force.

OPENING OURSELVES TO THE UNIVERSE

Read Walt Whitman's "Song of Myself." Read it aloud, over and over. He thinks his voice is the voice of "prisoners and slaves, thieves and dwarfs," "the deformed, trivial, flat, foolish, despised." He's everything, animate and inanimate. There are two movements: (a) opening ourselves to the whole universe as Whitman is doing, and (b) finding something of ourselves in everything and everyone, as Shakespeare is doing in both Hamlet and Iago. Hamlet is on the side of the angels, and Iago on the side of the devils, but to a writer's eye, there is something uncommonly common in the way the imagination operates in both these characters. It is interesting that Hamlet came before Iago.

Having considered one of the sources of energy in a writer, let us turn to a concrete instance of how any occasion can stimulate a writer. A person tells me the following episode. "I'm writing my first love letter. My mother wants me to go to the bakery and buy some bread. She says all she has is a twenty dollar bill. It's the end of the month. Twenty dollars is all she has till payday. I'm finishing the letter. I place a stamp on the envelope; as I lick the flap, I notice that the envelope I borrowed from Mother carries her perfume. I rush to the mailbox. At the bakery, I notice I've mailed the twenty dollar bill, and taken the letter to buy bread." This incident from another person's life stimulates me to think of dozens of events in which the main object of focus was a letter.

EXERCISE:

- Find movements from:

  - Innocence to experience.

  - Familiar to unfamiliar.

  - Knowing to not knowing.

With few exceptions, great stories are about human beings, but we know characters on a page differently from the way we know them in real life. The eyes of the artist see things differently. The artist is like the child. (S)he is aware of the mystery at the heart of each and every event. The child in Whitman's poem asks, "What is grass?" He brings a handful of grass to the poet. The poet can't answer. Perhaps, says the poet, the grass is itself a child. The writer doesn't give us answers; he fills us with awe and wonder. Literature does not teach us how to live. It is not a manifesto, or a program for a better life. Literature wakes us up, makes us aware, makes possible a free play of the mind, makes concrete the hidden part.

SENSATIONS

Each day we should do a few sensation exercises. Touch, taste, sight, smell, and sound. This creates immediacy on the page. But we want each thing to do double duty. Each sensation gives some depth to character or situation. We must not forget that we are entertainers. To some extent we must seduce and entice our readers. This works at every level. For example, reading Ibsen's *A Doll's House*, one is tempted to run out and buy some macaroons and brew a pot of tea. The realism or naturalism of nineteenth-century literature has many such details of the good life which are contagious. But the comfortable scene of tea and macaroons does double duty since it is related to the irony of Nora's situation, for she lives in a tenuous bubble which is about to burst.

MEMORABLE MEALS
EXERCISES:

- List memorable meals. Focus on smell, touch, sight, and sound. Omit taste.

- Think of a time you did not relish food or drink.

- Think of a meal with your first love. Focus on an object.

- Think of a meal that was eaten in silence.

- Think of the ugliest meal you ever ate. Focus on objects.

- Order the very last meal on earth for yourself or for someone else.

- A meal a person cooked that caused a problem.

- A time when there was no food. What happened next?

- Think of some period in your life when a great deal happened. Focus on a time when you had to give up something for a good reason.

```
             MORE SENSATIONS
   TOUCH
   TASTE
   SMELL      OBJECT        AND A PERSON
   SIGHT
   SOUND
```

EXERCISES:

- Make a list of all the people you know well, and put next to each name their weakest and strongest sense. Look for objects in each instance.

- Choose a short segment of time, a taste, a person, and a problem. A time when someone did not like his or her favorite treat. Avoid explanations.

- Smell and a person of the opposite sex. Smell and a person of your own sex. Focus on an object.

- Focus on real/unreal. Use touch, taste, and smell and alternate between objects or places that are real or unreal.

- Think of light/dark; focus on touch and smell and sound, that is, all the senses except sight which are directly related to places that are light and places that are dark. Alternate between light and dark and focus on an object.

AVOID EXPLANATIONS

If we listen to ourselves, we will find certain patterns, echoes, rhythms; these will be basic movements and basic emotions that recur. There is an individual way of putting things which is intrinsic to the telling. This voice is recognizable, like the timbre or accent of our speech or the pattern of our thumbprints.

The fiction we write is an exploration of personality. One person's wonder and sense of mystery awakens us by putting us in touch with the pluses and minuses in an event. At the heart of every image there is a mystery, something that resists paraphrase. As fiction writers, we must refrain from explanations that would deprive the movements in our fiction of this depth and resonance.

In order to practice the pace, choose a short segment of time when something big happened, and then after writing that, choose a longer segment of time when nothing happened. Learn to speed up and slow down. Accordion-style, open some up and compress others. Tell orally a sequence of events as rapidly as you can. Choose the basic emotion, "fear"; think of an event. In some parts use an accelerated pace, and in some parts use slow motion.

PRIMARY IMAGES

Each of us has a crucial event, which we think changed us more than anything else. We think of this event as the key to our whole life, as if it has colored every other event. You need not mention this event, but look at the people present. Separate them into three columns; the ones you like, the ones you don't like, and the ones you have mixed feelings about. Now think of objects that come to mind when you think of each of these persons. See which of the objects will open up into a movement. The lesson we learn here is an important one. Pain sharpens our perceptions.

OPPOSITES

No one would normally see "a great cathedral bell" and the "labels of jars of cream" as having something in common. Yet, in Part I, Chapter 9 of *Madame Bovary,* Flaubert yokes these two objects together in one sentence and echoes his meaning on the next page with the use of the word "halo." Emma is awakened by the visit to La Vaubyessard. Contact with aristocratic life left upon her heart "a waking that would never wear off." It is a new religion. To dress and look like an aristocrat, she sacrifices every consideration, getting deeply into debt to the sharklike Monsieur Lheureux; the word Paris, the world of all she aspired to, "dinned in her ears like a great cathedral bell, it flamed before her eyes like the labels on her jars of cream."[2]

---

2. Gustave Flaubert, *Madame Bovary*, Alan Russell, trans. (Penguin, 1983), pp. 69-71.

PREWRITING EXERCISE:

Think of Miss Havisham's mouldy wedding cake in *Great Expectations* by Charles Dickens. Think of all the people you know, and make a list of objects they have held onto in an attempt to freeze time.

EXERCISES:

- PURSUE / FLEE   COMFORT / DISTURB

  FIND / LOSE   CLOSE / DISTANT

  CONSERVE / DESTROY

Think of these words and think of situations between people. Put down an object for each. Write two scenes, one about the first meeting between two persons and another about the last meeting. Follow the sequence as it enters the mind. Focus on tangibles. Do not explain anything.

- OPAQUE / TRANSPARENT   ROUGH / SMOOTH

  THICK / FLIMSY   TIDY / UNTIDY

  HARD / POROUS   BRITTLE / SUPPLE

Without thinking or editing, put down objects that come to mind when you think of these opposites. Write single lines about each and save.

- SWEET / BITTER   FRIGID / PASSIONATE

  ACCEPT / REJECT

Brainstorm for objects that come to mind when you think of these opposites. A time when you said, "I'll never fall in love again," but did.

- CLOSE / DISTANT   SOFT / HARSH

  NEAR / FAR   DIRECT / INDIRECT

Think of these words and think of a person involved. Think of these words and think of a person in love. Think of something that happened between them that caused a problem. Make a list of objects that come to mind. A lover's quarrel; alternate between direct and indirect speech.

DONATING

EXERCISES:

- It's time that we began to share some of our insights. In order to do this, choose a person other than yourself, who felt what you have felt at one time or another. What is the difference? Feel the difference. Focus on an object. See the place. Who else is present? Write down rapidly what comes to mind, as if you're telling it to someone else.

- Take an event from your life, and give it to this person you were thinking about in the above exercise. Donate it. Give him or her objects that are related to a basic emotion in your own life. As fiction writers we must think of the events we have experienced as a kind of blood bank from which we will give transfusions to our characters.

- Look over everything you have written so far. Read it aloud into a tape recorder. Listen to it; see if there are adjectives, adverbs, explanations, or intrusive adverbial phrases. Remove them wherever possible.

TENSES

In the first half of this program, we write in the present tense so as to remove the clutter and to prevent explanations. But after we have learned to focus, we begin to translate our images into the simple past. Study the tenses in Hemingway's story, "Indian Camp." When in doubt, rehearse in the present tense and translate back into the simple past.

EXERCISES:

- Get in touch with sensations: touch, smell, sight, and sound, related to food. Go back to childhood. Think of a place and a time and a person. You may use the simple past.

- Think of your strongest sense and your weakest sense. Think of a time when your weakest sense felt like your strongest. Focus on objects. Feel the basic emotion.

- Make a list of strange noises you heard in the middle of the night. Think first of customary or habitual actions and think of that one time when something unexpected happened. Think of a movement from familiar to unfamiliar.

- List all the times when you thought your sense of smell was a burden. Think of object, place, person, event, and segment of time. Write very short movements.

- Through your five senses, focus on natural objects and being in love. See something strange that happened to a person who was in love.

- List things that look good but taste terrible, and vice versa. Think of people who look great but turned out to be disappointing, or vice versa.

FOOD, CLOTHES, AND SLEEP

Food and clothing may be overriding fashions in real life, but they seldom take a proportionate amount of space in fiction (food and wine punctuate the narrative of Hemingway's *A Moveable Feast*). For our purposes it is enough if we keep an illusion of the presence of these natural appetites, except when there is a dramatic necessity in focusing on a particular item of clothing or food. (See *Madame Bovary* for the dramatic use of clothing.) Similarly, a character might sleep a third of his life, and dream every ninety seconds of sleep time. In fiction we refer to sleep tangentially. We must never forget we are entertainers. The narrative pace is what determines success or failure.

MAKING LISTS

From time to time, we make lists: we move away from the abstract and we try our best to make them as tangible as we can. These are prewriting exercises. They are a vital source from which will flow some of our best images. Supposing you were to make a list of all the times you lost or misplaced money. Next to each entry, you would try to brainstorm for person, place, event, segment of time. Even if you didn't immediately write it out into a unit of narration, it will gather force in your subconscious and become a part of your fictional vocabulary.

Although these lists appear in one section of the manual, it is recommended that they be attempted one at a time, rather than all at once. Lists may be made once a week, or once a fortnight, depending on how much time you are giving to your writing.

THE INVISIBLE WRITER

PREWRITING EXERCISES:

- Go back to childhood. Make a list of all the objects that come back to you when you think of a dark place. Pick the ones that would have been bright if the light was better.

- Make parallel lists of people you wish were your relatives and people you wish were not your relatives. Find objects for each person.

- Make a list of things you overheard without the speakers knowing that you did. Find objects for each instance. A secret that everybody knew, but no one was willing to talk about.

- Make a list of all the times when people you consider sane have done crazy things. Focus on objects. A crazy person who made sense to you but to no one else.

- Make a list of the moments when people who cared for you did not act in your best interest. Find objects in each instance.

- Make a list of basic emotions and under each emotion put down the names of persons who come to your mind when you think of that emotion. List the objects that come to mind when you think of these persons.

MORE LISTS

When making lists, avoid abstractions and labels. Remember that even though a person may be a *type* and things (s)he does may be *typical*, (s)he is one-of-a-kind and the event is a one-time action. The object you focus on is also one-of-a-kind, something particular, that will stand out, like the tobacco case Madame Bovary brings home from the ball.

PLUSES AND MINUSES

PREWRITING EXERCISES:

- Make a list of the things that gave you pleasure and the things that gave you pain. Focus on an object, place, person, and event. Choose in each instance a short segment of time.

- Make parallel columns, one with objects related to "good" and the other with objects related to "bad." Remember, you're a storyteller. Find objects that are *both* good and bad.

- Look for objects that have both a plus and a minus. See which of them will open up into a telling. Make a note of each.

MOVEMENTS: SEE A MOMENT OF CHANGE BETWEEN:

STRANGE	→	FAMILIAR
PRETTY	→	UGLY
SERIOUS	→	FRIVOLOUS
REAL	→	UNREAL
SEXY	→	FRIGID
MAD	→	SANE

After making lists, come back to them and see which ones will open up. Make guide notes. You can't step into the same memory, in the same way, unless you make notes. Each time it surfaces, it's different.

PREWRITING EXERCISE:

- Brainstorm for impressions of new things, both man-made as well as natural, for example, a new baseball, a litter of kittens, fresh-cut pine trees at Christmas time, grass growing between and under stones. Keep closely observed objects for use as background in stories.

HEROES AND VILLAINS

- Make a list of your "heroes" in mythology, in history, and in public life. Look for people in real life who resemble these. And then look for a flaw in each person.

- Make parallel lists and divide people you know into those who give help and those who take help. Find a person who gives help but finds it hard to take any, or a person who takes help but finds it hard to give any. Find objects. A do-gooder who could not manage his/her own life.

Along with these personal images, find public events as background for the story.

PREWRITING EXERCISE:

- List all the public events that left an impact on you, on people you know, on the town or city you have lived in.

> THE HERO IS RESPONSIBLE FOR THE ACTION IN THE STORY.

FALLING IN AND OUT OF LOVE

Falling in love or breaking up are the most common themes in fiction. Even the more realistic works of fiction have romantic quasi-religious overtones when dealing with this theme.

EXERCISES:

- List all the times you've been in love. Put down objects for each time. Look for objects with a plus and a minus. Write the ones that will open up.

- Make a list of all the kinds of people that you could never be in love with. Put down a one-of-a-kind object for each of these persons. Find those objects that have both a plus and a minus. A person in love who flirted with everybody.

LISTS AND OBJECTS

EXERCISE:

- Think of objects that come back to you from a time when you were in love. Divide the objects into two columns according to pleasure and pain. Look at the objects; feel the emotions. One of these entries will open up into a telling in which something happened that changed everything. Write the ending. Do not explain anything. Consult the last three lines of Hemingway's *A Farewell to Arms* as a touchstone. Notice how the objects suggest the emotion to the reader. Set it aside for a while and then write the piece.

WORK AND PLAY

The days are gone when characters in fiction could be having tea, or riding to hounds, just being ladies and gentlemen of leisure. American fiction, particularly as befits a democracy, shows characters to be professional or working persons. Mark Twain had a bit of fun in *Tom Sawyer* where he points out that what is work for one character is play for another.

WORK

EXERCISE:

- Make a list of jobs or professions you have had. Think of a repetitive pattern at work. Choose different segments of time. Focus on place and person and event each time. Let there be a short break on the page between scene and scene. Let the reader deduce the irony or pattern.

LOVE

EXERCISE:

- Make a list of all the common features between someone you knew in childhood and a person you were in love with. A repetitive pattern in love. Choose different segments of time when a similar sort of thing happened. Look at each segment with a one-of-a-kind object as a one-time action. Let the reader see the repetitive pattern. Do not explain.

WORK

○ Make a list of all the professions you know intimately—sewing, cooking, carpentry, gardening, etc. What's work for one person is play for another and vice versa. Make work and play lists.

MONEY

For me, money is a medium of exchange; what is it for you?

○ Make a list of all the times when there was no money and focus on the objects for each instance. Think of the first money you earned. What happened next?

○ Make parallel columns of people you know well who are either richer or poorer than yourself. Find objects that show the difference. Set aside for later use. Think of a person too rich or too poor to fit in.

FORM: A REMINDER

As things surface, make quick notes—there's an order in which things surface and it is good practice to note down the sequence. The very act of putting down the sequence will teach you more about creative fiction writing than any course you've taken in writing. The form in which things come to you is original; that's *your* voice, as unique as your thumbprint.

SHORT SEGMENT OF TIME WHEN SOMETHING HAPPENED

TOUCH

TASTE

SIGHT   OBJECT   PERSON   PLACE   EVENT

SOUND

SMELL

EXERCISES:

- Make a list of objects belonging to the family which were not valued and which later turned out to be very valuable. An object you hated that filled a friend with envy.

- Think of several generations in your family, or in the family of someone you know very well, and list all the local, national, or international events that have affected them. Put down the names of persons most affected. Find an object for each.

- If you thought of life as a battlefield, list all the wars. Make notes.

SECRETS

EXERCISES:

- Do not write it on the page, but go over in your mind all the secrets you never mean to tell anybody nor write about. Feel the emotion in each instance. Get in touch with the five senses. There's a possibility of donating one of these to someone totally unlike yourself. Someone who betrayed a secret that you told them.

- Make a list of all the times when someone told someone else something they shouldn't have. Find objects in each instance. Was there a neighborhood gossip? See the person. See a time when this person caused a problem or solved a problem.

LOVE

EXERCISE:

- A relationship that was ruined by relatives.

OBJECTS

EXERCISES:

○ Find objects for the following labels: unreliable, unreasonable, ignorant, angry, emotional, frightening, powerful, underhanded.

○ Think of all the things which you thought were disgusting but were actually attractive to you. Focus on objects in each instance.

○ Make a list of all the lies either you or someone else told. Focus on objects.

TIME

Time is of the essence in fiction. If you understand how time works in fiction, you will recognise *form* in what you write. Read "Eveline" in *Dubliners*, and figure out the use of time in it. What's the shortest segment of time which gives a hint of narration?

MORE ABOUT TIME

In a story called "Adventure" in Sherwood Anderson's *Winesburg, Ohio*, a woman waits fourteen years for the return of a young man who went away to Chicago to work on a newspaper. A close study of this story will teach us to handle longer segments of time without losing immediacy. Read and reread this story; mark all the "time segments" mentioned in the story. In the opening sentence, she's twenty-seven. Her age is echoed in the third paragraph. In the beginning of the fourth paragraph, we go back to when she was sixteen, to the prior problem. The middle of paragraph four refers to "late in the fall of her sixteenth year." The sixth paragraph opens with the evening before the young man left Winesburg. Likewise, work through the whole story and mark the building blocks as in the clothesline method, until you reach the image of the girl crawling on her hands and knees in the rain through the grass to the house.

EXERCISES:

- Stay with a particular period, a particular place; think of all the significant events that took place there.

    We are only interested in what happened next. Therefore, pick a segment of time: state the surface time.

    What is the depth time?

    How will you go back and forth, and what is the image within the image?

    Think of opposites in each instance and go after it; write rapidly without thinking. Take down dictation.

    SURFACE TIME   PROBLEMS   DEPTH TIME   CHANGES

    If your sentence comes out choppy, it means you are not listening to yourself. Do biofeedback and start again with another image.

- How many secrets do you have? Count them. Don't tell anyone.

TABOOS

EXERCISES:

- List taboos that made sense to you.

    Place an object next to each entry.

    Look at the ten commandments and look for moments when you or someone else broke one of them.

- List taboos that didn't make sense to you.

    Place an object next to each entry.

    See who else is present.

    Brainstorm for sensations.

THE THIRD THING

Wilfred Owen was born on March 18, 1893, and he was killed in action on November 4, 1918, a week before peace was declared. His early poems are imitative, but in the last year of his life he found his own voice. He would have been one of the great poets of the century had he lived, but as it is, he wrote some of the best war poems in the English language. We have a manuscript draft of a poem of his called, "He Died Smiling." In three quatrains, we see the attitude of each member of his family, and in the fourth and last stanza, we see the situation in the trenches. The pluses and minuses, the contrasts, scorch the reader. There is no message in the poem, but we feel the painful irony of the title.

HE DIED SMILING

Patting goodbye, his father said, "My lad,
You'll always show the Hun a brave man's face.
I'd rather you were dead than in disgrace.
We're proud to see you going, Jim, we're glad."

His mother whimpered, "Jim, my boy, I frets
Until ye git a nice safe wound, I do."
His sisters said: why couldn't they go too.
His brothers said they'd send him cigarettes.

For three years, once a week, they wrote the same,
Adding, "We hope you use the Y. M. Hut."
And once a day came twenty Navy Cut.
And once an hour a bullet missed its aim.

And misses teased the hunger of his brain.
His eyes grew scorched with wincing, and his hand
Reckless with ague. Courage leaked, like sand
From sandbags that have stood three years of rain.[3]

Each image has at least two problems and a third element. What is the third thing in the poem, "He Died Smiling"? What is the irony?

---

3. *The Collected Poems of Wilfred Owen,* ed. C. Day Lewis (New York: New Directions, 1965) p. 76. Copyright ©1963 by Chatto & Windus, Ltd. 1963. Reprinted by permission of New Directions Publishing Corporation.

OBSESSIONS

EXERCISES:

- List obsessions—yours and other people's. Focus on an obsession and see where it goes. Follow the sequence. Focus on objects.

- Make parallel lists of what you think are obsessions that make no sense to you and obsessions that make sense. Look for objects in each case. Find those objects that have both a plus and a minus. Open up one of the above and look for a movement from familiar to unfamiliar or from happiness to unhappiness. Write the ending without explanations.

THE CHAMELEON POET

John Keats spoke of the chameleon poet and the negative capability of the poet. He wrote in a letter to Richard Woodhouse explaining the writing self:

> It has no self—it is everything and nothing—it has no character—it enjoys light and shade; it lives in gusto, be it foul or fair, high or low, rich or poor, mean or elevated—it has as much delight in conceiving an Iago as an Imogen. What shocks the virtuous philosopher, delights the chameleon poet. It does no harm from its relish of the dark side of things anymore than from its taste for the bright one; because they both end in speculation.[4]

In our workshop we practice this. We provide material to stimulate the reader. It is the reader who judges.

Keats goes on to say that when he is in a room with people, the identity of every person in the room so presses upon him that he is "annihilated." He goes on to add that this happens not only in a room full of men, but a nursery of children. When we talk about the fictional method of turning the camera eye outward, we are being truthful to the way the creative self perceives the world.

---

4. Russell Noyes, *English Romantic Poetry and Prose* (Oxford University Press, 1956), p. 1221.

GETTING IN TOUCH EACH TIME

In order to get in touch with the creative energy inside us, we should empty our heads of all the clutter and do the biofeedback exercise. Then, almost wordlessly, having shed our presuppositions, we can enter the roomful of men or the nursery of children and see, touch, taste, smell, and hear everything and everyone in the room. There is no barrier between us and the outside. We are ingesting everything through our capacity to feel deeply. The five senses and depth of emotion are the capital of the writer.

It's important to make lists of the basic emotions that you have felt and brainstorm for places where you've felt them, for the people who call up these emotions and the objects you associate with these. Most of them will open up. Make rapid notes in your journal. These are notes that will go into stories later on. In order to become a story at a later stage, an idea or theme will attach itself to some of these notes. When that happens, listen to the process in which the sequence enters your mind and write it down as if taking dictation from a super-author inside your head.

Use words in such a way as to seem wordless. Avoid adjectives and adverbs wherever possible.

ON BECOMING THE INVISIBLE AUTHOR

When moving the camera eye outward, think of yourself as an invisible person. Nobody sees you; you're not visible, but you're there. There is a hierarchy. This hierarchy has nothing to do with the ordinary world where the president of the company, or the woman with the money, or the educated man might get more attention. In our story, it's the connection to the basic emotion that determines which character and which object is at the apex of the hierarchic structure.

DON'T NAME THE EMOTION

The basic emotion should not be directly mentioned or labeled. It's what people do, it's what happens next, that makes visible the emotion, the conflict, the idea, or the theme. Each thing we do on the page must move the story forward in terms of what happened next, whether it's description, or dialogue, or exposition. The narrative thread must advance. It is in this sense that character cannot be separated from situation. Our minds can move with great rapidity over a whole sequence of events. Writing is a manual skill. There is no recording device yet that can transfer the speed with which our minds conceive episodes and actions onto paper. Each of us must devise ways in which to catch it all in the order in which the camera eye inside us spans the time, the place, the objects, and the event.

OPEN-ENDED IMAGES

In real life, we have certain beliefs, religious or secular. They may be the beliefs of our family, or class, or race, or country. We have to be aware of these. We could sit down and make a list, and we could divide our life according to beliefs. Having done this, look for objects, and then put plus and minus against each of these objects. The most valuable objects have both a plus and a minus. We should see which of these will open up in order to tell about person, place, and event by focusing on the object.

In real life, we're imprisoned by our beliefs. We're locked within various systems. If you focus on objects that have a plus and a minus, our characters, our creations on the page, will have choices and freedom. They won't be pulled like puppets by dogma and creed. At the same time, we give our readers an opportunity to interpret, to feel, to enter the world we have created. The movements of fiction are open-ended in such a way that the image continues to resonate. The movements achieve completion in the mind of the reader. To each according to his ability, observe the free play of the imagination.

FAITH AND DOUBT

"Nature never did betray/ The heart that loved her."
—Wordsworth

Do you agree?

IS MAN A PART OF NATURE?

EXERCISES:

○ Make a list of natural calamities, and make a list of man-made calamities.

○ Think of man-made and not man-made objects that have caused you pain. Look for opposites.

○ A good person who did something terrible.

○ A person who betrayed his own beliefs.

○ Think of a person who didn't believe in having any beliefs.

○ A person who admired bad people.

ENDINGS FIRST

Choose a segment of time when something happened, and write the ending. Read it into a tape recorder. Remove adjectives, adverbs, and explanations. Write the beginning by focusing on an object and seeing what happened next, till you catch a moment of change. Read over the beginning, middle, and end. Remove the false beginning. Begin at the point which has no explanation or description and has a prior problem which needn't be stated but which will emerge out of what happens.

A REMINDER

"In life, a thief is bad and a murderer is worse; in literature, a thief is good and a murderer is better."

```
TOUCH

TASTE

SMELL      OBJECT: WHAT HAPPENED NEXT?

SIGHT

SOUND
```

EXERCISES:

- Think of a time when someone did something good or bad without meaning to.
- Think of a time when a person you believed in didn't live up to your belief.
- A good result from bad beliefs or vice versa.
- A moment when someone shattered something you believed.

RIGHT AND WRONG

EXERCISES:

- A time when you couldn't decide whether a person was good or bad. Tell about an important event in this person's life. Focus on an object.
- Think of a time when your sympathies were with an opponent of someone dear to you.

FALSE BEGINNINGS

Remove false beginnings: don't give the background of a story at the beginning. Plunge in.

EXERCISES:

- The beliefs of someone else that caused you a problem.

- A belief that didn't make sense until...

- A moment when you lost faith but found something.

CLOCK TIME AND STORY TIME

Try rapid telling of some events. The ability to expand and contract time can be learned by going over the stories in *Dubliners* and *Winesburg, Ohio*.

EXERCISES:

- An old person who was wise. Make a list of objects connected to this person. Look for pluses and minuses. Focus on an object that has both.

- See a person who is elderly. Move the camera outward and focus on objects. Make a list of one-of-a-kind objects. Find something that belonged to this person when (s)he was young, something that gives you an entirely different sense of the person than the commonly accepted view.

- A wise person who did something foolish or a foolish person who did something wise.

MAN IS A SPIRIT

Man is a spirit. This the poor flesh knows,
Yet serves him well for host when the wind blows,
Why should this guest go wrinkling up his nose?[5]
—Stevie Smith

Is man a spirit, or is he a body? Brainstorm for moments when either body or soul ceased to matter.

---

5. *Oxford Book of Contemporary Verse 1965-1980*, D. J. Enright ed. (Oxford University Press: 1980), p. 7. Reprinted by permission of New Directions Publishing Corporation.

MORE ABOUT BELIEFS

In a poem called, "Why Should Not Old Men Be Mad," W. B. Yeats seems to show that old men know things that the young do not know anything about, and therefore old men feel a holy rage against the tragic ironies encountered over a lifetime. It appears as though the old world places the elderly on a pedestal, but not so in the new world. Where do you stand?

EXERCISES:

- Divide your life according to beliefs.

    Look for objects in each division.

    Put pluses and minuses and look for ones that have both a plus and a minus.

    Choose an object from this list. Get in touch with the basic emotion, and write.

- Think of moments of faith and moments of doubt. Focus on objects.

ACTOR TO WITNESS   PART 4

ACTOR TO WITNESS

In the beginning of this program, we write images in which the narrator is the actor. We look for sensation, object, place, event. And we ask ourselves, "Who else is present?" Touch and taste and smell are the private senses, sight and sound are the more public.

EXERCISES:

- Go back to the very first exercise, mother and a pleasant smell and a basic emotion. Now pick a person other than yourself who has come up in a subsequent exercise and give this early memory to this other person. See what happens next.

- Hear sounds you heard as a child, and give them to another character, in another time.

DONATING AND CREATING COMPOSITES

EXERCISES:

- Use one of your parents as the parent of another character. See what happens next. Focus on an object.

- Look for an event in your life that you've never been able to tell anyone about, and look for another town as a setting for this event. Change the sexes of all the characters. Focus on objects.

- Take your earliest memory and place it inside an event that occured much later—learn to put two segments of time together which are united invisibly by the same basic emotion.

- Choose an event in which you were at the receiving end and reverse the roles. For example, if a woman was betrayed by a man, write a story in which a woman betrays a man using the same objects and material as the original.

- See a person other than yourself feeling something you felt before. What is the difference? Focus on an object and tell what happened next.

- Think of a situation now that recalls something that happened a long time ago. Move from the present to the past and back again to the present. Avoid contrived transitions; the mind of the reader makes the connections—give the reader some work. Feel the emotion but do not directly name the emotion; allow the tangibles and what-happened-next to suggest the emotion. Do not try to make it into a "*story.*" Read over what you have written and remove all contrived transitions.

- There is a person in your life who enters your mind often when you are talking to others. This person seems to take up more space in your mind when you are with other people. Make a note of the kinds of things that come to mind about this person. Set it aside; you may want to donate some of these entries to your fictional characters later on, as the need arises. These real-life entries are a sort of blood bank for your future fictional characters. Note down direct quotes of what this person said that keep popping into your mind.

- Think of a relative you have heard a great deal about, but whom you have never met. Think of something that happened that no one wanted to talk about. Focus on an object and tell what you know about it. Do not explain; see what connections you can find between what happened in a private and a public event.

READING AND REREADING STORIES

As in poetry, some stories have a rhythm from certain repetitions (echoes), as in *Winesburg, Ohio* by Sherwood Anderson. These echoes build a pattern of expectation in the reader. To internalize this technique, read and reread Anderson's story, "Hands," untill you can retell it in the sequence in which Anderson wrote it.

OBJECTS

EXERCISES:

- Think of objects that have existed in the family before you were born. Look at a photograph of a member of your family from before you were born. What do you see? Is there something that tells you something about a person or event? Focus on an object. In a good telling, there is a revelation.

- Something you notice in a photograph that you had not noticed before.

LOOK FOR REPETITIVE PATTERNS IN LIFE

EXERCISES:

- A mother who competed with her daughter or a father who competed with his son, or an intimate antagonist.

- Think of fear. Focus on objects like a poorly lit street, a machine that was misused, lipstick on a lover's shirt. Look into situations that come readily to mind and find the object.

- An event that happened that colored other events. Focus on an object.

- An unreliable person who kept falling in love with reliable persons, and vice versa.

RHYTHM AND CLUES

By planting certain clues and motifs, we create in the reader a pattern of expectation based on it. For example:

- Choose a short segment of time: focus on a place you escaped to when something happened. What happened next? Don't try to make a story out of it. Feel the moment. Focus on the clearest object and follow the sequence of what happened next.

A place of refuge, once established, can begin to have a resonance all its own when referred to again. Anything connected with this place can immediately alert the reader—such a signal to the reader can be a wordless source of meanings that change the movement in which it recurs.

EXERCISES:

PRIVATE: TWO UNITS OF TIME

- Think of a person whom you once liked, but who has been a problem since. Think of a good moment with this person and then think of the worst moment—see if there is any connection between the two. Focus on an object and tell what happened each time.

PUBLIC:

- A world event that affected a small place. Focus on objects. Find objects that have both a plus and a minus. See the person or persons. Follow the sequence of what happened next.

- Lift your eyes from the enclosed space of home and look outside. Look at the neighborhood, town, city, country, continent, hemisphere, our earth, and so on.

Follow the order in which things surface in your mind. Listen to yourself.

EXERCISES:

- Pick one person who has been a problem to you but whom you have been fond of. Think of the worst moment with this person and think of the best moment, and see if there is a movement from pleasant to unpleasant.

- Two persons who stayed together even though they hated one another.

FOCUS ON AN OBJECT

- A family feud and a missing object. Focus on the object, tell what happened, and *stop*. Don't go on with it.

- A conflict between two siblings. Focus on an object. Do not explain anything. Stop when it's still going strong.

- A quarrel over property or inheritance.

BASIC EMOTIONS

Look up the difference between "jealousy" and "envy" in the dictionary. Brainstorm for objects by going up and down your life. Have you forgotten your siblings? Where are they? Go up and down the events and find objects for "envy" and "jealousy." Envy is over *things* or *objects*. Therefore it is easier to brainstorm for objects. Jealousy is over persons. Jealousy is a *grand* literary emotion; find objects to focus on when dealing with an event that has to do with feeling jealous.

EXERCISE:

- Two rivals in love with a third person at a dinner table. Focus on an object over which there is conflict.

If you don't find an object, make a note of the entry, and look for another event around an object, e.g., a car, a coat, a gift, a memento from a past event with the third person. Life is full of tangibles that cause problems. Be careful not to address the emotion directly. Let the reader do the work of judging the nature of the basic emotion. Do not explain the action.

EXERCISE:

- Think of a time you expected to feel jealous and didn't.

Do not make things reasonable or logical. The heart has its own logic, different from the brain. In writing, we follow the logic of the basic emotion.

EXERCISE:

- Make a list of all the times you felt jealous. Look for objects to focus on.

OBJECT — PLACE — PERSON — EVENT — SEGMENT OF TIME

EXERCISES:

- Think of a person who, to get out of one bad situation, got into a worse one of another kind.

- Think of a time when you or someone else started out on an adventure and it turned out to be a misadventure.

- Think of two enemies who became friends and turned against you.

- Think of the end of a relationship.

- A tragic event that ironically turned beneficial.

EDITING

PART 5

EDITING I

After writing an image, set it aside for a while. Meanwhile, try to narrate it, without benefit of the text, to anybody who'll listen to you. Listen to yourself as you're telling it. Go back to the written version. See if it is close to the oral telling. The idea is to write lean, to give the illusion of wordlessness. Remove any straining for effect or preciosity. Be particularly careful about the beginning. Learn to hook the reader's attention in the first line. Remember that your first sentence is competing with thousands of competitors for the attention of the reader. The opening line should put the reader into the main movement of the story, without preamble or prologue. There should be no elaborate, descriptive setting-up of the scene. Most beginners try to explain the circumstances that led up to the main event. Strike out such false beginnings.

EDITING II

Look for an object that opens up the main movement. See if the focus is right in terms of the rest of the story. The opening of "The Sisters" focuses on a lighted, square window. The opening of "Hands" focuses on the half-decayed veranda near the edge of the ravine and a fat, old man walking up and down nervously. In both stories, the beginning and the end of the story give us time present, and the middle of the story gives us time past. The prior problem is embedded in the story, the story does not begin with it. See that the ending has objects in it and no explanation. Mark all the objects in your image; question the ones that have no real function. Do not rewrite, merely question it. What you have learned, you will put into your next image. There is a wealth of images yet to be discovered.

EXERCISE:

- ○ Underline all inanimate objects in stories. Circle those that have a function, other than creating space on the page. Highlight those with a dramatic function, that is, the object may be connected with the moment of change.

EDITING III

Look at all the verbs. When an image is not well focused, or lacks immediacy, rehearse it in the present tense. Such passages can be easily translated back into the simple past, which is the usual narrative tense. Underline all the verbs. Question the past-perfects and the pluperfects. See if any of them can be moved to the simple past to give more immediacy on the page. See how many of the verbs can be action verbs. Action verbs give more muscle and energy to a movement.

Look at each of the verbs and see if they are in active or passive voice. Avoid too many boring verbs.

Occasionally an active verb can be used to suggest passivity, as in "Eveline." For example, in the first sentence, it's the evening that's invading the avenue. In the second sentence, she doesn't *lean* her head against the dusty curtains, her head *was leaned*, and the dust *was* in her nostrils (*invades*.) The third and final sentence of the paragraph, "She was tired," suits her static situation. Linking verbs and the passive voice can be used to advantage in such situations, but generally we want verbs that have a more dramatic connection with the subject and object. A good sentence has in it a minimal plot. A good sentence has in it recognition, reversal, and change.

EDITING IV

Go over the image and see if there's any dialogue. Notice how little dialogue there is in the story "Paper Pills." In fact, the only direct sentence is a mocking one uttered by Dr. Reefy. This is directly related to the theme of the story. Dr. Reefy writes images like we do. He doesn't share them with anybody. He just writes them on scraps of paper, and rolls them up into little balls, which he dumps on the floor. Here Anderson uses the storyteller's method.

EXERCISE:

○ Study Jane Austen, E. M. Forster, and Hemingway for dialogue.

There is a metaphor in the middle of "Paper Pills," the little twisted apples that grow in Winesburg. There is a core of sweetness in these apples that only a few people know about. The story of Dr. Reefy and the tall dark girl, and the paper pills is like these twisted apples.

EDITING V

New writers have a tendency to subsume certain sentences by making them dependent clauses, or adverbial phrases, and so on. If the action in a dependent clause is the main focus, it's best to rewrite the sentences by giving each clause its independence. At such times, the simple use of the word "and" restores equal weight to sentences of equal dramatic importance.

There is no need to begin each sentence with a noun. Joyce begins the second paragraph of "Eveline" with the words, "Few people passed." A beginning writer might have said, "Eveline saw that few people passed." In fact, it would be a good exercise to go through Paragraph Two of "Eveline" and mark all the sentences in which Eveline is not mentioned directly even though it's told from her point of view.

Just as a story has its hierarchy of significant, more significant, and most significant details, or objects, or characters, or gestures, so also every sentence has what is known as *emphasis*. Think of the most important noun or verb in a sentence as being under stage lights.

DIALOGUE

Try to create an illusion of complete speech with selected direct speech rather than *everything* you heard someone utter.

In the beginning we may not have too much dialogue in our writing, but as we begin to write longer images, we learn to work with passages in direct speech. Occasionally, we may give the illusion of direct speech, even though it is written indirectly. Look at the story, "An Encounter" in *Dubliners*. Read several times the second half of the story beginning with the paragraph in which we find the boys in a field. There they meet the queer stranger. The man delivers two different monologues. His perversity and obsessive manner are brilliantly caught. This is a good model to imitate while trying to compose a dramatic monologue.

THE USES OF DIALOGUE

CORRESPONDENCE BETWEEN MR. HARRISON IN NEWCASTLE AND MR. SHOLTO PEACH HARRISON IN HULL

Sholto Peach Harrison you are no son of mine
And do you think I bred you up to cross the River Tyne
And do you think I bred you up (and mother says the same)
And do you think I bred you up to live a life of shame
To live a life of shame my boy as you are thinking to
Down south in Kingston-upon-Hull a traveller in glue?
Come back my bonny boy nor break your father's heart
Come back and marry Lady Susan Smart
She has a mint in Anglo-Persian oil
And Sholto never more need think of toil

You are an old and evil man my father
I tell you frankly
Sholto had much rather
Travel in glue unrecompensed unwed
Than go to church with oily Sue and afterwards to bed.[1]
—Stevie Smith

We've become aware of the uses of dialogue. When there is a head-on conflict between two characters, a scene in fiction is closest to a well-made play. At other times, a phrase or a direct quote—a snippet of conversation—can give an illusion of dialogue, as if we are in the presence of a speaker, even though we are giving only significant phrases (see "The Catbird Seat"). We cannot use in a story all the direct speech uttered by the originals of our fictional representation. We don't generally use dialogue to advance story line; there are more economical ways of doing that. We listen to the voice inside us, notice how it speeds up, slows down, and jumps over segments of time. Listen to the pace; we are taking down dictation. Go back and study "The Sisters." Sometimes we see characters as less than ourselves, and sometimes as more than ourselves. Donate to the least of your characters a bit of yourself.

In dialogue each character must be true to his or her own emotion. (S)he must hold on to his or her own basic emotion from a prior problem which is not the same for any two persons. Each must avoid the other's script, and keep to their own individual "ancient history." They must turn their seeing outward and focus on something outside their own selves that both can touch or kick around or put away, something that is tangible. For dialogue to work in conflict, each must shut out the other's script and go on with their own, till the moment of change. Stop immediately—don't go on and kill it with boring post-mortems.

1. Enright, *The Oxford Book of Contemporary Verse*, p. 5.

EXERCISE:

○ A moment of conflict over something trivial. Focus on two persons. Put down what each said to the other. Look up dialogue in your favorite novel for punctuation. The least distracting form of credits is "Tom said," Mary said," "he said," "she said."

TOUCHSTONES

Matthew Arnold introduced us to the idea of touchstones, but he was thinking of touchstones or yardsticks for critics or readers. We are thinking of touchstones for our writing selves. Particularly, we want the best openings and endings from great works of fiction.

Each new writer should have at least one novel or a few short stories that he knows backward and forward as a kind of touchstone. We should read a passage from it every day and learn as much as we can. When we say *learn*, we mean learn the craft, the various tricks that create an illusion on the page. Study beginnings and endings. Study how short movements fit into longer movements. Study dialogue and dialogue credits (he said, she said). Study the way the camera eye of fiction moves, how the narrative pace is quickened and sometimes slowed. Notice how on a good page each line does more than one thing. Something may advance the storyline while at the same time building the atmosphere. Notice how the writer abstains from explaining, and most of all, notice how inanimate objects have a dramatic function in terms of storyline while at the same time they are connected to the basic emotion of the particular movement in which they appear.

For example, in *Madame Bovary* (Part 2, Chapter 8), Emma Bovary gives Rodolphe a nudge. (They have not yet begun their affair.) A beginner writer would have given away the reason for the nudge, but not Flaubert. He makes Rodolphe wonder, "What's the meaning of that?" This gives the narrator an opportunity to focus the camera eye on Madame Bovary, and she is seen through Rodolphe's eyes. About ten lines of that puts the reader in the middle, between them. Then, "Is she laughing at me?" Rodolphe wondered. After that, Flaubert permits Emma to explain why she nudged him: Monsieur Lheureux is trotting at their heels. He is there at the inception, and he is there at the close, and it is he who is the active agent in Emma's final circumstances. His presence here implies that Flaubert already knows how the story will end.

POINT OF VIEW

Point of view is related to the basic emotion. Action is related to the basic emotion. The objects too. It is the emotion that gives unity to a telling. Go over the past months and make a note of the basic emotions you have touched upon. Which ones have you left out? Make a note.

EXERCISE:

- ○ Put down basic emotions, the ones you have not attempted. Find objects for each. Find the place, the persons, the event. Choose a segment of time; break the segment of time into shorter segments. Choose the tiny segment which constitutes the ending. Start writing the ending. Read out the ending. See if a listener can get the movement, the emotion. See if there are any explanations. Remove the explanations. Remove wordiness. Is it open-ended, will it continue to grow in the mind of the listener? Now write the event. Go back to the beginning and see if you can remove explanations; see if there is a hint of a problem or mystery or conflict, or any kind of hook to make the reader wonder what happened, and what happened next. Read out the whole.

We hang up our short images on a clothesline, and we take them down when the ink is dry.

The length of a piece has nothing to do with the duration of the action. *Ulysses*, by James Joyce, is about a single day, Bloomsday. Take the total unit of time and break it up into shorter units. Each of these shorter units may be seen as a shorter movement or scene. Do not explain the connections between scene and scene; the reader does that. Remember how little poets and playwrights explain.

After a while, two or three units on the clothesline join hands together mysteriously, and they become larger units of narration.

As soon as an image surfaces in your mind, determine how much time the episode took in clock time, then see if this segment of time which is the largest unit of time can be further divided into shorter segments of time. Certainly, there is the prior problem, which forms a unit by itself. There is the unit which makes up the ending. There is the unit of time when something changed, after which things were not the same as they were in the beginning. These short movements are each capable of standing by themselves, and yet, because they originally surfaced in the mind as one event, the basic emotion will cast over this whole series the quality of being indivisible. In most cases, we do not begin with the prior problem. If we did, it would sound like an explanation. The complication will come out in the course of the telling.

EXERCISE:

- An event you wish you could relive to make amends. Choose two segments of time, one containing the event and the other a consequence. Focus on an object each time.

PLOT

In "The Catbird Seat" by James Thurber, we begin with a mystery object, the Camel cigarettes, and then we proceed to the prior problem of the previous week. From there we go to the accumulated problems of the past two years in the immediate past. You will notice that these segments that give us the prior problem also establish the character of the protagonist. Each block of narration must do more than one thing. Mr. Martin's reliability is established indirectly. Any direct statement about the character from author to reader would (a) spoil the illusion of immediacy, (b) take away freedom from the reader, and, (c) make character and situation static.

How does James Thurber establish the reliability of Mr. Martin? How do we know it's not a case of paranoia? We're given snippets of dialogue from the boss and two assistants. The glass of milk in his hand is not only related to his character, but also to the plot, the climax of which occurs in Mrs. Barrows' apartment, where Mr. Martin asks for a scotch and soda. The catastrophe for Mrs. Barrows occurs in Mr. Fitzweiler's office, where the reversal of fortune takes place. She's no longer in the catbird seat. At that point, she recognizes how Mr. Martin has tricked her by staging an act. But the true reversal is that, at this point, the victim becomes the victor.

The remarkable thing about the story is that it is clearly making fun of the Aristotelian plot while at the same time vindicating the Aristotelian plot for the marvelous thing it is. We never quite forget surface time, and each "place" in each block of narration is closely tied to the action; plot and character are inseparable, as in any well-made play. We notice the animal imagery; the donkey, the horse, the rat, that turn up in human guise, but these suit the antiheroic nature of the story.

Contemporary antiheroic writers think they have broken with Aristotle. They think their stories have no beginnings and endings, only suspended middles. Such stories claim to be the children and grandchildren of Dostoevsky's Underground Man, but if we were to re-examine Dostoevsky's *Notes from the Underground*, we would find that the narrative units within the two parts can stand by themselves. They have a basic emotion, they focus on objects, place, and person, and they're framed by a specific unit of time. Of course, we would have to ignore the polemic and look for narrative images.

The polemic itself is no ordinary polemic. The narrative tension is built up through the device of establishing a dramatic relationship between the speaker and the listener (the listener is the reader), so that the reader becomes a powerful polarity, a sort of antagonist, who will be left shaken at the end. The incident with Zerkov, or the two separate scenes with Liza, produce the pluses and minuses that are essentially paradoxes which the reader deduces as he would in real life. Part Two of *Notes from the Underground* is a conventional narrative. In Part One, the reader enters the narrative as a presence to challenge the active narrator and make him shift, revise, and reformulate his views. Without the reader's participation, the so-called "Notes" would be the suspended middle it claims to be.

It is possible to have a structure without a traditional plot. But the smaller units within the larger structure have a unity of time, place, and action, and may be said to have "plot" in that sense.

IRONIES AND PARADOXES

Camus' novel, *The Stranger*, is a direct descendent of Dostoevsky's *Notes*. In Part One of *The Stranger* we are with Meursault every inch of the way. We experience what he experiences. What we experience in Part One is the immediate. In Part Two, the witnesses for the defense, in spite of their best intentions, cannot represent Meursault's reality on the witness stand. It's the tension between Part One and Part Two that lifts the story above the ordinary. For the purposes of the clothesline method, it is worth examining the story-within-the-story in the newspaper clipping that Meursault finds in his prison mattress.

"The paper was yellow with age...it was the story of a crime." So it begins. A man from Czechoslovakia left home to seek his fortune abroad. He returned with a large fortune and a wife and a child. His mother and sister were running a small hotel. He put up his child and wife in another hotel and went and stayed incognito at his mother's place. That night, he flashed around a large sum of money. That night, they killed him with a hammer, and after stealing his money, they threw his body into the river. Next day, the wife came, and the identity of the stranger was revealed. The mother and sister killed themselves. What is the relationship between this image and the larger image of the stranger, who is condemned to death not because he killed an Arab in self-defense (it was no crime for a white man to kill an Arab in French Colonial North Africa) but because he failed to weep at his mother's funeral?

Non-Aristotelians have traditional units of narration in their shorter movements, and these go to make the longer units. The shorter movements within the longer units are held together by causal connections. This is so because these things are fundamental to the way we perceive. Even a well-formed sentence with an action verb may be said to have a plot.

It is generally believed that all we have are material objects, and that all we have is the present. Yet, if we were to close our eyes and try to evoke a physical impression of our own bodies, we have no physical image of ourselves except for the flat reflection in a mirror. In our dreams, when we dream we are dead, we either wake up or we continue to dream and we see our own funerals. What does this mean?

To ourselves we are not physical entities, and the human mind cannot accept temporality. The old belief in the soul and eternity is intrinsic to the way the mind perceives and has nothing to do with religion or superstition.

In fiction, the spirit is made incarnate, the intangibles come to us through the tangibles.

We make no distinction between the traditional and the modern, the material and the spiritual. Good stories focus on object and place and person and event. They use the particular, the one-of-a-kind objects to suggest the universals that are common to everyone everywhere.

Traditional units of narration may be seen embedded in the so-called "experimental" writing.

EXERCISES:

- Get in touch with your five senses. This is to be done daily, like practising five-finger exercises. Tell a short movement through the five senses.

- Use your senses and think of a movement about spring. Now think of an opposite that comes into your mind. Note it down. Feel the basic emotion. Look for an object, and by focusing on this object you will be able to give us a movement with the basic emotion, something that can stand by itself. Something your listener can enter. See who is there; look at the place. Feel the atmosphere. Move the camera outward. Focus on what is happening next.

- A painful flaw in someone you or another person loved. Focus on an object.

- An event that occured between you and this other person that colors everything else that happened. Usually there is a whole series of things that happened. Let it flow down your hand and through your pen onto the page.

- Brainstorm for parallel columns of things about this person that made you feel unsure of yourself, and the things about you that made the other person unsure of himself/herself. Look for objects in each instance and write short movements.

- Make parallel columns of people you love and people you hate. Find persons you both love and hate. Like and dislike. Look for objects. Look for plus and minus.

- Prewriting. Make new lists. Getting in touch with sensations: think of moments when it was difficult to say anything; get in touch with a dominant impression through one of your senses. Focus on an object each time.

- Each of us has a primary wound. Find yours and note down sensations and look for an object that had a part in what happened.

- It is believed that things don't really have an impact on a person except when this wound is reactivated. Think of a creative moment when pain led to something out of the ordinary.

- Think of a moment of exorcism, when the old wound healed and you did not find yourself caught by the old hook. Now think of something new that entered your life.

AUTOBIOGRAPHY VERSUS FICTION

Fiction invents the lie that tells the truth. Fiction is not merely what happened, it is the tension of opposites, the pluses and minuses which belong to the characters whose emotion gives unity to the narration. Readers are not interested in your life story. In fiction there is work for the reader. What the fiction writer sees, no one else would have seen in that way. In this, it is different from a news item in the papers. Fiction can be read and reread, and each time the reader begins to see something that expands in the mind and wakes him or her up.

Fiction comes out of life. At the same time, we are storytellers. These two go together in our writing. If we merely thought of our experiences, we would be writing true confessions, memoirs, diaries, autobiographies. Fiction is experience *plus something else*. This something else is a many-splendored thing. But at its most basic, it's a primitive art of keeping the audience hooked to the narrative thread, which is the what-happened-next.

Fiction comes out of a subconscious level that is free of interferences, and the narrator finds himself freer than in real life where (s)he is bound by duties and habits.

We have learned that we need both the plus and the minus in any single image. We need the contrast. As one participant said, "Endless sunsets stop being noteworthy. Boring. A rainy day sets up a rainbow nicely. The plus needs a minus."

EXERCISES:

- A very short segment of time when something changed / altered, when something *happened*.

- A very short segment of time when something happened, told rapidly.

- A very short segment of time when something happened, told slow motion.

- A very short segment of time when what happened resisted your understanding.

- Find objects for the following movements:

FAMILIAR / UNFAMILIAR	HAPPY / UNHAPPY
INNOCENCE / EXPERIENCE	PASSIVE / ACTIVE
FAITH / DOUBT	VICTIM / VICTOR

- Think of opposites: find tangibles for each pair of opposites, from a moment in your life when something happened. Remember, we have an open mind, and our reader should know how it feels.

CHOOSE A SHORT SEGMENT OF TIME WHEN SOMETHING HAPPENED

TOUCH

TASTE

SMELL   OBJECT   PLACE   PERSON   EVENT:
WHAT HAPPENED NEXT?

SIGHT

SOUND

"SLINGS AND ARROWS OF OUTRAGEOUS FORTUNE"

- A person who performed his/her functions well, but had a problem that no one could help him/her with.

- A person who felt a lot at a public event, but did not feel anything for a private situation.

- A person whom you fell in love with who reminded you of one of your parents. Focus on an object.

- A time you mistook someone else for one of your parents, or vice versa. See a feature, an item of clothing, a gesture, a statement uttered by the person.

- An object you associate with someone in authority who was immature.

- Think of an object you associate with a survivor.

- Meeting a person who was/is the lover of someone you love.

- Think of a fair-weather friend and a moment you got help from an unexpected source.

- Think of a time when two persons were having a fight and you got mixed up in it.

- A moment when someone felt abandoned or isolated. Focus on object, place, person, and event.

TURNING A PERSON INTO A CHARACTER ON A PAGE

- Think of someone who suffered a loss and behaved in a theatrical way.

- A person who boasted of things that another person might have been ashamed of.

- A person who was sensitive who behaved insensitively toward another.

- A person who had power over another person. Focus on an object he used to control the person.

- A quarrel between two persons over rival beliefs.

- Think of a person who would do anything to be in the limelight.

○ Think of a child who was not innocent.

○ A pathetic person who entertained on a grand scale. Focus on objects.

○ A man who hated women or a woman who hated men.

○ A woman other women didn't like, or a man other men didn't like.

LISTEN TO THE SEQUENCE AS IT SURFACES IN YOUR MIND

○ A person everyone liked but you did not like.

○ A person most people disliked, but toward whom you felt sympathetic.

○ Think of a person who was utterly unattractive, but had a lot of power.

○ A powerful person who would not help.

○ A person who helped another, ignoring his/her own interests.

○ A person who took pleasure in another's failure.

○ A person who was self-destructive.

○ A person whose life was ruined by someone close to him/her.

○ Think of a parent who was badly treated.

○ Think of a person without sight who saw a lot, or a person with a handicap who did a lot.

UNIVERSALS AND ONE-TIME EVENTS

- A person who could not hear good things said about him/her.

- A person who was unfairly prejudiced against another person.

- A person who changed completely in the presence of another.

- A person who didn't keep a promise or a person who couldn't make up his/her mind.

- Think of a person who was completely familiar who did not understand you. Focus on objects.

- A miser who did something generous or a generous person who did something miserly.

- A person you admired doing something ordinary, or a person you thought poorly of doing something extraordinary.

- A person who had everything except freedom.

- A person who ran away from a situation.

- A person who was misplaced or displaced.

- Think of a time when someone you know well was blamed for something (s)he did not do. Don't try to cram everything into this one image. Another image will do for another aspect. Later these short images will fall into place and become a longer sequence. The manner in which this happens is a mysterious process. The short images you are surfacing will now activate energy which will bring forth more and more material. We are doing five-finger exercises.

- A familiar person who looked strange suddenly. Go back to childhood, to a time when there were many mysteries. Do not explain. Choose a short segment of time. Let the entry be no longer than a few lines. But feel the movement as intensely as you can; record it through your senses. Avoid abstractions.

- Think of something that someone left behind that caused a problem. For example, a piece of furniture that couldn't be disposed of, a will that caused anger. . . . Focus on objects.

○ MENTAL-PHYSICAL / ACTIVE-PASSIVE

CAREFUL-CARELESS / TIDY-UNTIDY

Think of places where you worked and put down names of persons who come to your mind when you think of these jobs. Put down an object next to each. Think of a sequence of events related to a work situation in which either jealousy or envy created a problem. Do not explain. Use no adjectives or adverbs. Write the ending first. Do not begin with the prior problem. Let it emerge in the course of the telling.

○ Think of a person who was not practical, but who had good ideas.

○ An innocent person who had powerful enemies.

○ A situation in which two persons joined together against a third person.

○ Someone who was trying to make up for something that was not his/her fault.

○ A person who put his/her creative energy into their house.

○ Something you knew about a person that you wish you hadn't known.

○ An explanation that led to a misunderstanding.

○ List objects you associated with someone who was a mystery to you.

○ A moment when someone was angriest. Focus on an object.

○ An object a family associated with a war. Look for one-of-a-kind, one-time objects.

Most of us write in the head, we rehearse, before putting pen to paper.

EXERCISES:

- Look over your material and mark the basic emotions that recur. Notice whether the movement is from pleasant to unpleasant or vice versa.

- Find a theme that's running through several episodes or events. How would you put this theme in a sentence as an idea? Practice by putting into a single sentence the idea or theme of your favorite novels or stories. Make up one for your story or novel.

- Go over your material once more, rapidly, and think in terms of a beginning, middle, and end in each instance. If you're writing a novel, select and arrange roughly these events, that idea, and the sequence.

- Write the ending. There should be no explanations. Focus on an object. Feel the basic emotion. Remove any adjectives and adverbs. Strike out any explanations. Look at the ending of *A Farewell to Arms*. Read the last three sentences.

- Go over your material and find a moment that you think is the most important moment in the story or novel. Look for a change in the event for better or worse. Focus on what happened next. Write it down rapidly.

- Go over this event. Who are the characters in it other than yourself? Arrange the characters in a hierarchy of importance. Look through your exercises and select images and movements which you will donate to these, to each according to his need.

- Go for a long walk. As you're walking along, rehearse in your mind an opening scene for your novel. Ask yourself, what is the basic emotion in this scene? Who are the people in it? Focus on an object. Get in touch with your senses.

LOOK FOR SHORT MOVEMENTS

○ Tell the first chapter orally. Listen to the way you're telling it. Remember, you are a storyteller. Resist the temptation to explain. Think of the technique as seen through a camera eye. Focus on an object.

○ Go over the first chapter. Look at the verbs. Use the simple past. Use active verbs wherever possible. Listen to the rhythm of the sentences. Put it aside. Tell it again orally. Focus on what happened next.

The ending of a chapter should make further movement not only possible, but necessary. Yet the basic emotion gives the chapter unity and the focusing on object, place, person, and event makes the episode capable of standing by itself.

○ Block out, as you would when rehearsing a play, the rise and fall of the action. Write an outline as to what goes in where. Familiarize yourself with your material. Go back and forth until you find all the links in the chain.

Hemingway advised that we should quit each day when the writing is still going well, for then it will continue to ferment in the subconscious, and the image will pick up energy at the next sitting.

Individuality is not possible if there are no differences between characters. It's through conflict and separation that a person becomes visible on the page. What is the conflict? Look for objects.

In fiction, a character does not have to be rational or logical. But the sequence of events must have a logical connection in terms of consequences if the reader is to take it in. This is the logic that gives rise to what we call an action. Draw a graph of this action.

You are about to begin to write your first book. Do not stop to revise. Edgar Allen Poe said, "A long poem is a contradiction in terms. A long poem is but a series of short poems." There is a mysterious force inside us that knows how to make these units into an indivisible whole.

READING AS A WRITER

FIRST READING: LOOKING FOR OBJECTS

While writing, we read stories not as readers, but as writers. We're looking at a story to see how it is constructed. In a way, we're taking it apart phrase by phrase and putting it back together. We do this first of all by looking at objects in the story. Our first task, when looking at a story, is to circle inanimate objects in the story. We then notice that some objects are more important than others in the telling of the story.

In our own writing, we have found that focusing on an object helps us to open up a movement. We want to trace this process in the stories we read. Just as we don't want any description for its own sake, we don't use objects merely because T. S. Eliot said we should. We need objects to create fictional space. Without objects there is no space for the reader to move around in. We select objects that have a dramatic function. When reading stories, however, we should mark objects that have a dramatic function in a different colored ink, to distinguish from objects that don't have a dramatic function. For example, the handkerchief in *Othello* has a dramatic function.

SECOND READING: LOOK AT THE VERBS

At the second reading of a story, we notice the tenses. Immediacy is the first criterion. At the very beginning we may use the present tense so as to remove clutter of different segments of time, and to help focus, but in the hands of a more experienced writer, the simple past tense gives us this immediacy.

Next, we look at the verbs and see which of the verbs are active and passive and which of the verbs merely link subject with object. In our own writing we are not overly conscious in our first draft of whether a verb is active or passive. We don't actually stop to think how many action verbs there are in a movement. If we are faithful to the voice inside us, there will be a direct relationship between the voice of our verbs and the voice of the storyteller. But when we *read* a story, we examine every verb.

THIRD READING: BEGINNINGS AND ENDINGS

At the third reading, we look at the beginning and we look at the ending. For example, in the story called "Araby," Joyce begins with a street, North Richmond Street, which we are told is blind. At the blind end (the word "blind" appears twice in the first paragraph) there's an empty house that stands "detached from the rest." This is in contrast to the other houses where people live "decent lives." But these houses "gazed at one another with brown imperturbable faces." Having understood the first paragraph, we look at the final paragraph.

In the final paragraph of "Araby," the narrator is "gazing" into the darkness. He is alone. He is at a dead end. He is like the empty house that stood at the blind end. (Others may look at one another with imperturbable faces, but his eyes "burned with anguish and anger.") It's a moment of illumination, and he sees himself as a "creature driven and derided by vanity." It's not only Richmond Street that's a dead end, but perhaps Dublin, too, and innumerable other cities the world over. The sentence marks the end of childhood, but it's a childhood that we never free of the taint of experience. Wordsworth thought that heaven lies about us in our infancy. Joyce did not. What do you think?

FOURTH READING: PATTERN, RHYTHM OF EXPECTATION, AND ECHOES WITHIN ECHOES

Having understood the beginning and the end, we go back to the rest of the story and we notice that the girl, Mangan's sister, is a body, a physical presence. She's definitely not a soul, but a body, and the self-condemnation in the last sentence of the story ("a creature driven and derided by vanity") prefigures the earlier sentence, when he says that "her name was like a summons to all my foolish blood." The spirit of adventure and the lure of the exotic (the syllables of the word "Araby") take the narrator nowhere. He is let down. There are "intolerable delays," and when he arrives at the magical bazaar, he sees a weary looking man who takes his shilling and two other men counting their coins. What he hears is the fall of coins. One would mark all the mention of money—pennies, shillings, etc.—in the story.

FIFTH READING: MARK THE UNITS OF NARRATION

We learn to divide stories into parts. These parts are the movements or images on our clothesline. We see how the author composes these short movements and then fits them together to make a larger whole. And we remember the wisdom of Edgar Allen Poe's remark that a long poem is a contradiction in terms. A long poem is but a series of short poems strung together. Short images add up. We may not immediately see the connection between various items on the clothesline, but in some part of our consciousness, the connections build arches and make different movements come together, to make an organized whole. We should never ask of an image, what use is it? In some extraordinary way, the usefulness will present itself to us.

SUMMING UP

If we were to look back, we would find that we listened to ourselves when we were little. Generally, mostly under favorable conditions in nursery school, others, particularly the teachers, listen to the voice of authority within the child. Nursery school education believes that the child is king, but soon after that the confidence in the inner voice is eroded. The growing child (the storyteller in the child) is placed somewhat in the position of a copywriter with a client that must be satisfied. For many crucial years thereafter, authority seems to lie outside the child.

One participant who is a successful commercial filmmaker says, "The simple reason for that is that there are clients, people who will, willingly, and without any sense of what they are doing, dismember your idea in the service of their perceived wisdom or knowledge of the subject area. After you get chewed up a couple of times that way, you learn that *you are not the authority* and that you must destroy your nerve ends about what you write and produce."

These things need to be emphasized and re-emphasized. Listen to yourself. You are the authority. Follow the sequence in which something surfaces. We must tell and retell our stories orally till we hear our own voices. What we're listening for is that voice we had when we were in nursery school. If we can *hear* ourselves, then we learn to hear other people. As Eudora Welty says, we not only listen to stories, but we listen *for* stories, meaning, we learn to recognize beginnings, middles, and ends.

One of the first discoveries we made in this program astonishes most of the participants. Writing can be fun. If we feel any pain in surfacing conflict, the pain quickly turns to pleasure and a sense of power unlike in real life where conflicts may pull us down. Focusing on objects and building on what-happened-next makes the emotion that was a minus in life a plus on the page.

In reminding ourselves that conflict is necessary to create individual consciousness in a story, we are turning the slings and arrows of real life into a powerful source of energy in our creativity. This has a liberating effect. We remember: in real life a thief is bad and a murderer is worse, but in literature, a thief is good and a murderer is even better.

WAKING UP THE READER

Why do we sound negative? Tolstoi began *Anna Karenina* with the words, "All happy families resemble one another, but each unhappy family is unhappy in its own way." This sentence contains within it the aesthetics of the novel. Consciousness is not possible unless one is separate. Separation is painful! Without the pain of separation, there is no individuality. It is when the mother withdraws her breast from the infant's mouth that the pangs of separation are first experienced. We need to re-experience these separations. What is unpleasant in real life becomes pleasant in the writing. This is the first step toward finding your own voice.

Our business is to wake up the reader. It is for the reader to exercise his judgment. We write in such a way that choices are possible for the reader. If our movements are not open-ended, the reader has no work. We focus on one-of-a-kind, one-time action. We focus on an object through which we begin to feel the basic emotion and we follow it where it takes us. As writers we say to ourselves, "Nothing human is alien." As beginners, *we* are the center of our images. But as we become more experienced, we learn to share the spotlight with other characters. Fiction writing is the act of moving the camera eye outward. We are witnesses. We make visible on the page that which is hidden in real life. But we do this by focusing on objects. We learn to become omniscient witnesses.

We begin to move the camera eye. We learn to move from being an actor to being a witness. From inside to outside, one season to the next, one person to another, one country to the next. We learn the full range of what we can do on a page by combing the real world for dramatic objects and persons and events. As fiction writers, we cannot move too far away from the real world; we have to create on the page the illusion of a real world with real frogs and real gardens. Unlike the historian, we have to be both universal and particular at the same time, and we have to make visible that which is not often visible to the mere reporter of events. Our strategies have come out of the modern preoccupation with realism. Even if we mean to write escapist fiction, we must learn our craft by taking something that is concrete and particular and translating it into that which is universal.

During the transition period between first-person and third-person narrative, we may alternate between being actor and being witness. At this point, we learn that each sentence need not begin with an "I" or a "he" or a "she"; we become aware that behind the character is the author. We begin to be able to create a little bit of distance between author and character.

As our voice strengthens, we learn to parcel out some of our own choice material to suitable recipients on the page. Eventually, we learn to share in this fashion with characters whom we may perceive as less than ourselves.

APPENDIX A

BIOFEEDBACK

Before we start writing, we do relaxation exercises. The words of the biofeedback exercises given below may be put on a tape, or you may memorize them. It is important that you do not vary the words. Each workshop session begins with five minutes of biofeedback.

Please sit in a comfortable position, preferably at your desk. Listen to the words.

- My right hand is heavy. (Three times. Feel the heaviness in your hand.)

- My left hand is heavy. (Three times. Feel the heaviness.)

- My right leg is heavy. (Three times.)

- My left leg is heavy. (Three times.) (Imagine the sun shining on your hands and feet.)

- My hands and feet are warm and heavy. (Six times.)

- Heart beats calm and regular. (Three times.) (Think that you are on a warm and sunny shore, and as the waves come in, you are breathing in from the diaphragm, and as the waves go out, you are breathing out.)

- It breathes me. (In = the waves are coming in. Out = the waves are going out. Three times.)

- My solar plexus is warm. (There's a warm grid of nerves, just above the small of your back. Feel it getting warm. Three times.)

- My forehead is cool. (Feel something cool on your forehead. Three times.)

- Fist your hands. Folding your arm at the elbow, raise your fist. Relax.

NOTE: For relaxation, repeat the above three times. (It takes 20 minutes to do biofeedback.) When in a hurry, do it at least once to clear your head. If you omit the last step, you will fall asleep.

APPENDIX B

READING LIST

- *Winesburg, Ohio*, by Sherwood Anderson.
- *Dubliners*, by James Joyce.
- *50 Great Short Stories*, edited by Milton Crane.
- *Short Shorts*, edited by Irving Howe and Ilana Wiener Howe.
- *Madame Bovary*, by Gustave Flaubert.
- *The Norton Anthology of Poetry*.